T0015389

HENRY DAVID THOREAU

Henry David Thoreau

Thinking Disobediently

Lawrence Buell

OXFORD
UNIVERSITY PRESS

Oxford University Press is a department of the University of Oxford. It furthers
the University's objective of excellence in research, scholarship, and education
by publishing worldwide. Oxford is a registered trade mark of Oxford University
Press in the UK and certain other countries.

Published in the United States of America by Oxford University Press
198 Madison Avenue, New York, NY 10016, United States of America.

© Oxford University Press 2024

All rights reserved. No part of this publication may be reproduced, stored in
a retrieval system, or transmitted, in any form or by any means, without the
prior permission in writing of Oxford University Press, or as expressly permitted
by law, by license, or under terms agreed with the appropriate reproduction
rights organization. Inquiries concerning reproduction outside the scope of the
above should be sent to the Rights Department, Oxford University Press, at the
address above.

You must not circulate this work in any other form
and you must impose this same condition on any acquirer.

Library of Congress Cataloging-in-Publication Data
Names: Buell, Lawrence, author.
Title: Henry David Thoreau : thinking disobediently / Lawrence Buell.
Description: New York, NY : Oxford University Press, [2024] |
Includes bibliographical references and index.
Identifiers: LCCN 2023019539 (print) | LCCN 2023019540 (ebook) |
ISBN 9780197684269 (hardback) | ISBN 9780197684276 (epub)
Subjects: LCSH: Thoreau, Henry David, 1817-1862. |
Thoreau, Henry David, 1817–1862—Criticism and interpretation. |
Authors, American—19th century—Biography. |
Transcendentalists (New England)—Biography. |
American literature—19th century—History and criticism. |
Civil disobedience in literature. | Transcendentalism (New England)
Classification: LCC PS3054 .B84 2024 (print) | LCC PS3054 (ebook) |
DDC 818/.309—dc23/eng/20230719
LC record available at https://lccn.loc.gov/2023019539
LC ebook record available at https://lccn.loc.gov/2023019540

Printed by Sheridan Books, Inc., United States of America

CONTENTS

ACKNOWLEDGMENTS

This book has greatly benefited from the help of many people.

Heartfelt thanks to Frederick Buell, Richard and Barbara Forman, Robert Gross, Richard Higgins, and John Stauffer for their penetrating feedback on chapter drafts; and an extra measure of the same to David Hall, David Robinson, Laura Walls, Kim Buell, and Ronald Chester for their astute readings of the whole. Many more colleagues and friends helped along the way as my ideas took form with insightful exchanges, often much more helpful than they could have known at the time, among them Ray Angelo, Roberta Bienvenu, Shirley Blancke, Irene and Richard Brown, Denise Buell, Christine DeLucia, Sarah Dimick, Herwig Friedl, Reed Gochberg, Rebecca Gould, Rochelle Johnson, Stephanie LeMenager, Ronald McAdow, John Mitchell, Jenny Rankin, Robert Richardson Jr., Jacob Risinger, William Rossi, Aaron Sachs, Ken Sawyer, and Nancy and Donald Swearer.

Richard Brown and *New England Quarterly* editor Jonathan Chu first made me realize the potential timeliness of a new book on Thoreau by commissioning an essay-review for *NEQ* on the remarkable outpouring of Thoreau scholarship around the time of the bicentennial anniversary of his birth in 2017. Presentations at the University of Oslo, Cornell University, Harvard University, and the Harvard Forest in Petersham, Massachusetts, enabled me to try out and refine my thinking about Thoreau. Also very helpful in crystallizing my thoughts and helping me self-correct my weakness for prof-speak has been the chance to present my thinking at public forums of various kinds hosted by the Thoreau Society, the Thoreau Farm Trust, and First Parish Lincoln and Wayland.

For essential help in securing illustrations, and for general archival navigation, my thanks to Ray Angelo, to Anke Voss and Jessie Hopper of the Concord Free Public Library Special Collections, to Jessica Delaney and David Wood of the Concord Museum, and to Jeff Cramer of the Walden Woods Project's Thoreau Institute.

From start to finish this book has benefited enormously from the guidance of my proactive and generous-spirited Oxford University Press editor, Nancy Toff, who encouraged me to write it, helped shape its vision, provided wise and witty counsel along the way, and gave what I fancied a finished manuscript the most intensive and perceptive in-house review that a work of mine has ever received. I could not have asked for a better editorial team than Nancy and her associate Brent Matheny.

Chapter 1

Life and Mythmaking

Henry David Thoreau is one of the few classic American authors who has risen to the status of international folk hero, despite a life much less eventful than the likes of Benjamin Franklin and Mark Twain. His apotheosis happened gradually during the century after his death in 1862 and hinged chiefly on the influence of the two works for which he is best known: "Civil Disobedience" (1849) and *Walden; or, Life in the Woods* (1854). In the process, his one night in jail and two years of bivouacking in the woods near his home have acquired a mystique more durable than Lord Byron's philandering, Alexander Pushkin's duel, or the hunting exploits of Ernest Hemingway.

Why that outcome makes sense will take the rest of this book to explain, but the heart of the matter is the energy and originality with which Thoreau expressed himself about a number of fundamental concerns that have mattered to others since. What are the essential ingredients of a good life? How can personal integrity be reconciled with the demands of society and the state? Of what importance is nature to modern civilization? These were questions he pondered throughout his life. In that sense his life, thought, and writing are all of a piece, vacillations and self-contradictions included. Most of the writings to which he attached any importance took years to germinate, nearly a decade apiece for the only two books published before his early death.

Thoreau was born in 1817 in Concord, Massachusetts, a small town west of Boston that became absorbed into its expanding metropolis during his lifetime as the American industrial revolution advanced. He lived there nearly his whole life, mostly under the same roof with his parents and siblings. After graduating from Harvard, he was swept up in the Transcendentalist movement, a multisided intellectual and social reform ferment whose epicenter was Concord and whose leading spokesperson, Ralph Waldo Emerson, became Thoreau's mentor. That impetus prompted him to reject a conventional career and become a freelance writer of iconoclastic essays and irreverent memoirs of travel around the American Northeast; a radical political theorist and antislavery activist; and an idiosyncratically brilliant field naturalist and nature writer. During the last dozen years of his life, Thoreau wrote voluminously in all these veins, outgrowing Transcendentalism and developing a contrarian voice all his own. At his death in 1862 at the age of forty-four, the great bulk of that writing was still in manuscript, and Thoreau seemed fated to remain typed as an Emerson clone. A century later, his stature had eclipsed Emerson's. "The village crank" was now "a world figure," as one of his intellectual heirs declared.[1] The fame of *Walden* and "Civil Disobedience" had spread worldwide, and his most important manuscripts were either in print or about to be in the next few decades. Only in the 2000s, however, have Thoreau scholars begun to grasp the full proportions of this emphatic but elusive thinker.

One of the fundamental challenges that confronts Thoreau readers is how to understand the relation between the historical Thoreau and the figure of Thoreau that his writing presents. The two Thoreaus are both distinct and inextricable. Therein lies the biggest roadblock to understanding either. The problem is compounded by the challenge of resolving either one into a single image. The biographical Thoreau was a more than ordinarily paradoxical creature whose personality is as much disguised as revealed by the wealth of documentation, including the two-million-word journal he kept throughout his adult life. Scholars are repeatedly tempted to the extremes of premature closure or dithering equivocation. Nor does the first-person voice in Thoreau's writing stand still. It oscillates between forthright and elusive, confidential and standoffish, lyric and sarcastic, polemical and ruminative, documentary and impassioned, serious and sly.

Perhaps the most basic dissonance between competing images of Thoreau stems from his being a boldly independent thinker who was also a confirmed homebody. His writing, apart from letters to family and close friends, conveys an image of one who preferred to go it alone. It may come as a jolt to discover that *Walden*'s staunchly independent hero, as the book acknowledges in passing, regularly strolled back and forth from woods to town the whole time he lived there, since he makes so much of his cabin's pristine setting and the epic stakes of what might seem a comparatively risk-free venture in his hometown. A stream of testy dismissals of Thoreau's fraudulent claims of remoteness and self-sufficiency runs from his day down to ours.

To rush to judgment is of course a reader's right, but it is more instructive to understand how Thoreau's thought and actions came to take the shape they did and have managed to speak to so many. A good first step is to consider the implications of Thoreau's call to "live 'deliberately,'" his omnibus term—or mantra—for the aspiration behind the Walden experiment.[2] He seems to have had in mind a cross between Socrates's praise of the examined life and Buddhist mindfulness, not that he was consciously thinking of either. "To front only the essential facts of life," as he himself encapsulates: to simplify the terms of life by dispensing with the superfluous baggage of things and received wisdom and by attuning yourself to a state of mental alertness and intensity that moves you past the "mud and slush of opinion" to some bedrock reality of the spirit from which life can be reimagined afresh, free from the slog of "quiet desperation" in which he sees most people mired.[3] *Walden* dramatizes this vision of the fresh start at a moment-by-moment level in its evocation of the details of the author's woodsy life—as if "beholding life through a very powerful magnifying glass," Virginia Woolf wrote in a shrewd appreciation on the centennial of Thoreau's birth in 1917. "To walk, to eat, to cut up logs, to read a little, to watch the bird on the bough, to cook one's dinner—all these occupations when scraped clean and felt afresh prove wonderfully large and bright."[4]

Thoreau's vision of living deliberately is both attainable and demanding. You need not travel far. A modest physical separation can do just fine. The transformation from secondhand to firsthand existence requires few tools and little money. The hard part is the inner part, which is also the crucial part. That is what drives the next level of magnification: imagining the experiment as a quest of world-historical proportions undertaken at an immense distance from the everyday. Just what Thoreau means by this, however, is tricky to understand, let alone achieve. The mythic extravagance of a Thoreau passage may signal any or all of the following and more: the magnitude of the attempt, the thrill of success, the mismatch between reality and dream, and—trickiest—playful disruption of the mood of grand assertion that oscillates between sheer display and wry disavowal of his seeming hubris.

A single passage may start in one direction, then veer off in another—as in the sequence leading up to "live deliberately." It starts with a glowing tribute to summer mornings at the pond as invitations to archetypal simplicity, celebrating his daily bath as "a religious exercise" in the spirit of Confucian precept and ancient Greek Aurora-worship. "Morning brings back the heroic ages": so the speaker propels himself back into mythic time. But quickly that gives way to a very different kind of magnifying image, as absurd as the other was heroic, recalling the sound of a mosquito buzzing through the cabin affecting him as much as "any trumpet that ever sang of fame"—a veritable "Iliad and Odyssey in the air, singing its own wrath and wanderings."[5] Homeric aspiration morphs into Homeric hijinks, in a freakish blowup of sleepless camper beset by noxious insect. Such vicissitudes convey both a sense of the supreme importance of the quest at hand and the need to approach it in open-eyed awareness that ordinary mortals including himself will find it a stretch to sustain, achieve, or for that matter always regard with fixed solemnity.

Magnification of the stakes of the present moment, whether in solemnity or in fun, is a hallmark not only of *Walden* but of Thoreau's writing generally, whether in the prosaic form of a protracted chronicle of the dimensions of muskrat or turtle carcasses over a half-dozen journal pages, picturing his morning dips as a ritual enactment, or the kind of extended tour de force later in *Walden* that places an ant-fight witnessed during "the Presidency of Polk" on the same plane as the American War of Independence.[6] Such mental intensifications of the local landscape and his exploits within it became almost second nature for Thoreau from adolescence onward.

Almost as soon as he started writing seriously, Thoreau was drawn to ruminating back and forth between the near at hand and the remote in space and time. Concord fields and woods resonated with memory of the aboriginal dispensation, "the eternity behind me as well as the eternity before." The Native Americans who sometimes ranged through the neighborhood were "my Britains come to Rome." The river that wound sluggishly through the town loomed up as an Orinoco or a Euphrates. In other moods, "farthest India" seemed "nearer to me than Concord & Lexington."[7]

Why such musings, common enough for an intellectually inquisitive youth, developed into settled habit rather than fading away with other adolescent residues one can only guess. Part of the story may have been coming of age at a historically resonant moment for his community, when Concord was celebrating its bicentennial as New England's oldest inland town and raising a monument to the first victory of the American Revolution, when the patriots "fired the shot heard round the world," to quote the Emerson hymn sung at the monument's dedication by a choir that included Thoreau.[8] Or perhaps, conversely, it bespoke a kindred form of the self-conscious provincialism that later led novelist V. S. Naipaul to measure his native Trinidad by English norms and populate his early landscapes with Dickensian figures in a mix of irony and yearning. Doubtless it also reflected Thoreau's lifelong zest for narratives of discovery and travel that began at least as early as his college years. Another influence may have been the college experience itself: Harvard's neoclassical regimen of assigning students to revisit episodes from Greco-Roman history and literature in their essays and oratorical performances. Or the excitement of living in a place in the throes of transformation from country village to Boston suburb with connecting threads radiating out though the region and beyond.

None of these factors, if indeed they were such, would have taken hold had Thoreau not been a traveler more vicarious than literal at heart. He loved globe-trotting mentally and sizing up his more dutiful fellow citizens with ethnographic hauteur as a benighted tribe engaged in strange rituals of penance. But his actual journeys were few, mostly local, and like as not undertaken with mixed feelings, especially in later years. His standard excuse that he could not afford travel was sincere, but it masked an increasingly settled centripetalism. Apart from a few unhappy months in his mid-twenties, he never seems to have considered moving away from Concord apart from a few inquiries about school teaching posts after his local ventures folded.

Reinforcing his lococentrism was the bond of family. Thoreau's precariously middle-class parents, both from clans that had seen better days, sacrificed to enable him to join the then-minuscule fraction of white American youth to graduate from college. But when he showed no desire to enter a regular profession after two stints of schoolteaching, far from holding it against him they cheerfully embraced him as a permanent member of the household. Thoreau reciprocated by making himself as indispensable to them as they were to him, assisting with many do-it-yourself projects, such as fitting up a new family house at the time he was setting up his own at Walden and, more important, helping sustain the pencil-making and graphite-processing business his father had started when he was a boy and he himself took over upon his father's death. Indeed, his technological savvy proved crucial to improving the fortunes of that enterprise to the point that the family could finance its move to a more commodious house on Concord's Main Street, where he finished *Walden* in the roomy attic that became his base of operations for the last dozen years of his life.

Almost never does Thoreau mention family in what he wrote for publication, and seldom even in his journal. For that reason, it is all the more important at the outset of a book devoted chiefly to his thought and work to come to terms with the complex part family ties played in reinforcing the sense of gap between the literary-intellectual Thoreau's imagination of himself as a lone voyager through distant spaces and the biographical Thoreau's comparatively modest and temporary breaks from quotidian routines and entanglements. To conceive the first merely as a reaction to the constraints of the second is simplistic.

For one thing, the bond to family reinforced his feeling of embeddedness at the center of the universe that in turn reinforced his proclivity for measuring Concord, for better or worse, against any and all exotic places and times. That same sense of portentous entanglement also magnified the seismic impact of any disruption. The sense of high adventure that makes *Walden* shimmer and makes "Civil Disobedience" frame the author's night in jail as exotic time-travel to the Middle Ages had a solid sociological basis. In the provincial culture that clung to Thoreau's Concord, small deviations loomed large. In the 1840s, the proper place for a Harvard graduate in the eyes of the community was a town law office or pulpit, and the kinds of people who lived in shanties in the local outback were immigrant railroad workers and local riffraff. Moreover, in those days, historian Robert Gross emphasizes, "Nobody lived alone—nobody, that is, with any choice in the matter."[9] So Thoreau's removal to Walden would indeed have seemed to his neighbors as strange as an excursion to the antipodes.

That Thoreau's family, apart from a few grumbles from his aunts, seemed untroubled by his growing reputation as village eccentric may have been that they too were an independent-minded lot. Thoreau may well have had his own clan in mind, and some other Concord families too, when he mused that "a true family" was an "older and more venerable state" than the state itself; that "the state & the town should be a confederacy of independent families living apart from each other with his own territory."[10] His parents and siblings were also progressive in opinion, selective in committing to collective enterprises, but decisive when they did so, including times when conscience trumped orthodoxy. The alacrity with which Thoreau's mother and sisters joined the embattled antislavery vanguard—considerably sooner than he did—is a case in point.

His father's manner of conducting his affairs may also have rubbed off on Henry. In his remembrance, although John Thoreau Sr. struggled with financial difficulties for most of his working life, he never put gain ahead of product quality, nor did he let work keep him from indulging a penchant for casual reconnoitering of the local scene. His son took this combination to a further extreme. As *Walden* shows, he was a vehement critic of bondage to conventional work ethics who insisted that six weeks of labor a year can suffice to free a person for higher pursuits and, in many charming passages, pictured himself indulging at length in recreational pastimes and meditation. That helps explain his early appeal to Victorian readers of genteel background as well as the bemusing fact that one of the earliest members of the Thoreau Society was a bona fide vagrant by the name of Roger Payne who had written a book called *Why Work*? Yet Thoreau was at heart also a rigorous perfectionist both as a literary craftsman and in his other pursuits, including the land-surveying practice that proved in the long run the most crucial factor in recouping his local reputation from slacker to valued citizen.

Walden downplays this latter side of Thoreau in order to dramatize how downscaling can free one from the bondage of making a living and—duplicitously, some may think—omitting to mention that he got more writing done at Walden than ever before in the same length of time. But a passage in the concluding chapter inserted into one of the late drafts tells the real story: a fable of an artist in the imaginary city of Kouroo who labors for eons to fashion a perfect staff that when finished metamorphoses into "the fairest of all the

A portrait of an idealized Thoreau about the time of *Walden*'s publication (1854). By all accounts Thoreau looked more sturdy than handsome. Crayon portrait by Samuel Worcester Rowse, reproduced from *The Writings of Henry David Thoreau* (Walden Edition) (Boston: Houghton Mifflin, 1906). *Courtesy of the Walden Woods Project.*

creations of Brahma."[11] The tale speaks for the author's own literary ambitions. In practice he wasn't always so self-exacting. Sometimes he acquiesced reluctantly to editorial micromanagement, and on his deathbed he released with minimal revision a tranche of manuscripts, short and long, that had been in progress for years. But he had his own way entirely with "Civil Disobedience" and the two books published during his lifetime, *A Week on the Concord and Merrimack Rivers* (1849) and *Walden* (1854).

A 1906 map of Thoreau country in the mid-1800s by photographer Herbert Gleason, corrected in 2021 by Ray Angelo, whose key to the numbered places is posted at https://archive.org/details/herbert-gleason-thoreau-country-map-corrected. Angelo has also assembled a more comprehensive list of the remarkable number of local sites—fields, streams, thickets, swamps, rocks—named in Thoreau's *Journal* and often rebaptized with his own pet names: https://archive.org/details/thoreau-place-names. In this way, like a local Adam, Thoreau made Concord's landscape his own. *By permission of Ray Angelo.*

Walden confirmed the allegiance to the Concord region as primary country of the imagination that Thoreau had basically felt all along even as he continued to write up his excursions to farther-flung destinations. Attracted though he was to such globe-trotting works as Alexander von Humboldt's *Travels* and Darwin's *Voyage of the Beagle*, his own forte was an increasingly concentrated and granular interweave—in its own way even more intellectually ambitious and more subtly nuanced—of scientific, ethnographic, philosophic, and lyrical roaming to the end of transmitting the feel of place-immersion and its inexhaustible capacity for generating adventures of the mind.

The best short key to how this preference congealed and what it meant to him is his lecture-essay "Walking," a bravura performance composed while still at work on *Walden*. It is the one among Thoreau's several noteworthy contributions to the genre of meditative-descriptive hiking literature from Jean-Jacques Rousseau to Robert McFarlane and Rebecca Solnit that explicitly formulates a theory of walking. As such, it supplies the backstory and raison d'être of what *Walden* drolly calls traveling in Concord better than *Walden* itself: the life-routines and sense of larger stakes into which Thoreau settled after his sojourn at the pond and started the lifelong regime of long daily forays from home to out-of-the-way parts of Concord to which he largely devoted his daily journal entries from then on. Those rambles were driven partly by a growing passion for natural history investigation but reinforced by a deepening sense of bond to the wilder niches of near-home fields, woods, and swamps that was at once aesthetic, spiritual, and sensuous to the point of erotic. By a paradoxical logic perhaps only fellow lococentrics can fully understand, as Thoreau's familiarity with the surrounding landscape grew, so did the wonder of its minute variegations by the hour, day, weather, season, mood, and the sense of inexhaustible possibilities for discovery always in store. Even in a lifetime of so exploring the ten-mile radius around home "it will never become quite familiar to you."[12]

With a typical mix of vehemence and whimsy, Thoreau imagines his regime of afternoon "sauntering" as spiritual questing, playfully deriving "saunter" from *sainte-terre*, or Holy Land. A few hours' walk from his door can get him "to as strange a country as I expect ever to see." A single farmhouse unseen before can be "as good as the dominions of the king of Dahomey." He can easily, so he says, complete an entire walk without approaching any house or even "crossing a road except where the fox and mink do."[13]

The synergy of physical place and projective imagination transports the experiencer into "a nature such as the old prophets and poets Menu, Moses, Homer, Chaucer walked in." Thoreau then anchors this sense of mythic time to Eurocentric westwarding mythography, deploying the then-standard tropes of America as a nation of boundless natural richness with more gusto than usual for him. The needle of his inner compass "inevitably" points him south-southwest, like the proverbial course of empire and the settlement of the American hinterland then underway. "I must walk toward Oregon, and not toward Europe," following "the general movement of the race." In fact the biographical Thoreau's rambles took him in all directions, and he was more repelled by the irresponsibility and wastage of westwarding than he was excited by it. Sure enough, underneath the surface rhetoric here flows the even stronger current of the localist counternarrative whose force he had come to feel in his bones. As he soon begins to explain, "The West of which I speak is but another name for the Wild."[14]

The essay then proceeds to unfold the sensuous and the spiritual implications of this assertion. At the material level, the gospel of wildness means, for example, putting the labyrinthine biotic richness of Concord's swamps on the same footing as the charismatic landscapes painted by the likes of Albert Bierstadt and Frederic Church, and a declaration of affinity with the other-than-human life of one's surroundings that we would now call biophilia. That affective bond is reinforced by the moral conviction that not only is wildness of inherent regenerative value for persons and cultures, but also that the test of a culture's legitimacy lies in sustaining the natural bounty on which it draws. Thoreau's touchstone is not the flourishing settlement carved from virgin forest but "a township where one primitive forest waves above, while another primitive forest rots below." Wildness as a property in nature is not his only interest, however. Equally if not more so, wildness is a property of mind: the extravagance of imagination that modern manners suppress, thoughts that break the mold, the epiphanies open to us when we let ourselves see otherwise. As always, Thoreau drives home the idea with a farrago of vignettes and aphorisms. One comes closest to summing it all up: "A successful life knows no law."[15]

Thoreau's ethos of staying put and questing locally—*Walden*'s rendition of it especially—has inspired thousands of neo-Thoreauvian voluntary simplicity projects on all six inhabited continents, urban as well as rural, varying in austerity from a long-term reclusiveness far more spartan and remote than his to weekend getaway retreats. Thousands more have invoked Thoreau in defending commitment to place against the presumption that uprooting and mobility are necessary for a successful and fulfilling life, and in defending the right of the individual to resist social and political pressure and the integrity of natural environment in the face of industrialization and urban sprawl. None of this would have been possible had the biographical Thoreau been a "normal" or "well-adjusted" person. The sense of one speaking as a resident alien is crucial to the effect and the vision that gave rise to it. The edge of provocation that has kept his life and writing alive—as irritating to some as compelling to others—partly arose from an array of personal frustrations, setbacks, and idiosyncrasies that deserve a closer look.

The deconstruction of standard westwarding mythography and the ethnographic hauteur with which Thoreau skewered village proprieties was partly driven by a confessed misfit's vexation at being thought perversely contrarian that he was too thin-skinned to take in stride. He took satisfaction in staring down gawking locals who scoffed at the seeming pointlessness of wading around a swamp all afternoon, but he was also hypersensitive to being gawked and scoffed at. Hence the studious avoidance of people so charmingly related in "Walking."

Another half-hidden downside of Thoreau's zest for outdoor roaming was likely the sense of exercise as a necessity for body as well as spirit. The image of hardihood conveyed by Emerson and others, which was the face he himself liked to present to the world, masks a fragile health history. Tuberculosis cursed many New England families of the day including his and him. It dogged his brother, killed one of his sisters, and probably accounted for several mysterious bouts of debilitation from Thoreau's teens through his thirties. It also helped ensure his long decline and death after contracting bronchitis in his early forties, at a much younger age than most other major nineteenth-century American authors. The four-hour afternoon breakouts "Walking" celebrates almost certainly helped him live as long and as well as he did, all the more so because the Thoreau house was suffused with minute particles of pulverized graphite from the family business.

In other ways, too, *Walden*'s claim that most men lead lives of quiet desperation was partly autobiographical. The spectacles of the first era of mass politics in national history infuriated him: populist demagoguery, proliferation of time-serving bureaucrats, the encroachments of slaveholding interests with the complicity of northern elites. At a more personal level, Thoreau never shook off the fatalism that overcame him with the trauma of the sudden death by lockjaw of his beloved older brother, which produced a violent sympathetic reaction during which he experienced all John's symptoms, followed by months of torpor and depression. For a decade afterward well into his thirties, he was haunted by the sense of inability to settle on a fulfilling vocational path, a malaise probably intensified by survivor guilt at outliving a more popular older sibling and certainly by knowing himself a failure in the world's eyes.

Intensifying that dissatisfaction was an undercurrent of Wordsworthian regret for the loss of a spontaneous excitement in nature, in the moment, in the sense of the numinous he remembered having experienced more keenly in youth. Emerson likened Thoreau to Pan, the nature god who beckoned others into the green world to their delight or consternation. But he was also a Peter Pan, who at some level always clung to "the lost child that I am,"[16] and who never ceased to relish the company of children, throwing himself into their games and guiding them on excursions. At those times he dropped the mask of ironic reserve for a carefree and tender manner.

With adults outside the family, Thoreau generally remained on guard and discouraged intimacy, though he did gain a small circle of friends and admirers with whom, especially through the distant medium of letters, he could strike an air of easy urbanity when he chose. In matters of the heart, he was more prudish even than the stereotypical Victorian norm—which we now know was actually not so "Victorian" as once supposed. The dry judgmentalism with which he tended to express himself in public, and which his preachier passages show to an even greater degree, led many to think him cold. A local friend quipped that she would no more think of taking Henry's arm than the arm of an elm tree. Emerson's memorial address at Thoreau's funeral sums him up as a "hermit and stoic," epithets that have rung true for many, then and now, reductive though they were.[17]

Reinforcing this image of chilly austerity was the near invisibility of Thoreau's love life, combined with the turgid high-mindedness with which his writing broaches the subjects of sex, chastity, and marriage. Only twice is he known to have been smitten by women, in each case whetted by rivalry with another man: an early summer when he and his brother courted a woman who rejected them both, and a fondness for Emerson's wife Lidian that he himself pictured as platonic—like a "very dear sister," he told Emerson.[18] Otherwise, he was drawn at least as strongly to male as to female beauty, and much more to male companionship except for his sisters and a few women older than he whose minds he respected. In any case, whatever the cause—sexual ambiguity, inhibition, indifference, all, or none of the above—by his mid-twenties Thoreau was a confirmed bachelor with a settled preference for solitude complicated by chronic dissatisfaction at the gulf he felt between him and others, for which by turns he blamed them and himself.

Readers will doubtless always differ on whether to count Thoreau's afflictions and social outliership against him, or to esteem his achievements even more remarkable on account of them—and for having been in no small measure made possible by them. This book unabashedly takes the latter position. To linger momentarily on a single example, take Thoreau's love of nature. No Romantic then or since has rivaled the peculiar intensity of his responsiveness to the natural world, particularly the near-home haunts he came to know so well. To exclaim that "All nature is my bride," or "I fell in love with a shrub oak" on an early winter walk, was more than metaphor, more even than philia. It registers a sensory hyperexcitation that can only be called erotic or libidinal.[19] So too with Thoreau's exuberant reaction to all of nature's reds, from osier tips in early spring to the riot of scarlet color in the woods of autumn, or the delicious sensation of strolling up and down a river naked in midsummer. These were experiences not so much aesthetic as viscerally sensuous. Did "any Roman emperor ever indulge in such luxury as this?" he exclaims after one river walk.[20] Quite conceivably Thoreau's receptivity to natural stimuli was quickened if not originally engendered by bottling up emotion on other fronts. But if so, considering the impetus that gave to his work, and the fact that he died affirming he was perfectly satisfied with his life and regretted nothing, why should we regret that he didn't lead a more "normal" life, either for his sake or ours?

Chapter 2

Essential Thoreau

Walden and "Civil Disobedience" make logical gateways to Thoreau's art and thought for more reasons than one. He rose from obscurity in his own time to world fame in ours chiefly on the strength of their impact. Even among Thoreau scholars, who are quick to point out that "Civil Disobedience" and *Walden* are but a small fraction of his total output, they have always garnered the lion's share of attention.

"Civil Disobedience" and *Walden* showcase the two genres Thoreau favored in what he wrote for publication, the lecture-essay and the descriptive memoir. The relation between them was more reciprocal than antithetical. His essays are punctuated by anecdote, the narratives infused with disquisition. Each shows a lifelong partiality for converting personal experience into parable. "Civil Disobedience" and *Walden* also overlap in content, each gesturing to the other. *Walden* includes a sketch of Thoreau's arrest and incarceration, which occurred midway through his sojourn at the pond. "Civil Disobedience" underscores his reputation for keeping his distance by stressing how he fled town immediately upon release.

Yet the two also pull in opposite directions: confrontation with the status quo versus retreat to a space apart. As such they dramatize a fundamental ambivalence that Thoreau's readers have widened. Some are attracted especially to the political Thoreau, reckoning his interest in the natural world either a distracting slippage or a symbolic screen for satire. For others the essential Thoreau was the father of American nature writing, the proto-modern field scientist, the patron saint of modern environmentalism and/or voluntary simplicity. Such disagreements have also fluctuated across place and time. In late nineteenth-century America, Thoreau was admired chiefly as a nature writer. His journal was first excerpted in four volumes of seasonal observations (*Early Spring in Massachusetts*, etc.) and his books promoted as "outdoor" literature. Meanwhile, Thoreau the social and political reformer attracted much greater interest in Britain and elsewhere abroad among such readers as Tolstoy, Gandhi, and the Fabian Socialist Henry Salt, author of the late Victorian biography that remained the standard life of Thoreau until the mid-twentieth century.[1] Later, predictably, the political Thoreau came into high fashion during the 1960s, and the late 1900s saw a rise of interest in Thoreau the proto-ecologist and environmentalist.

To what extent did Thoreau feel called to a life of action, whether social protest or useful service, to what extent called to pursue a course of solitary contemplation, of self-fashioning, of nature study? He himself wrestled with the question throughout his adult life. Whether those disparate tendencies can be resolved into a unitary composite image or whether they plunged him into irretrievable self-contradiction every reader must decide. To discuss "Civil Disobedience" and *Walden* side by side allows us to trace both the tensions and the interplay by focusing on major common denominators of his thought and art. Let us start at the level of core convictions and then move to matters of style and form.

The most fundamental affinity between "Civil Disobedience" and *Walden* is the preeminent value set on individual integrity. Both conceive individual persons as rightly and inherently free-standing agents and the alternative view of people as essentially social beings as a threat to that integrity. In everyday life, the threat is perpetual. One's core integrity, one's worthier self, is always at risk of erosion by direct pressure to conform and by one's internalized dutifulness. So "Civil Disobedience" deems unthinking execution of the responsibilities of a good citizen to be a slippery slope to moral asphyxiation, and *Walden* argues that men forfeit their humanity by dutifully laboring to acquire possessions they do not need. Thoreau loves to state the predicament in the most provocative terms: "What demon possessed me that I behaved so well?"[2] The embattled soul who would preserve integrity and spiritual well-being is pitted against the vast majority of those around him who, without malign or even conscious intent, conspire to thrust him into inauthenticity or keep him there by the inertial force of expectation and behavior.

"Civil Disobedience" and *Walden* both turn on breakout moves made by the author under conditions of duress that are conceived both as idiosyncratically personal and as typifying pressures that other persons of conscience must face. Each builds the case for liberation from false consciousness by boiling down the work of government or of livelihood to bare essentials, so as to unlock the inner energies released by following conscience or genius despite what others think and do. For *Walden* this means devoting the first and longest chapter to defining the essential ingredients of "economy" or physical sustenance: food, fuel, clothing, shelter. Scaling down to the level of actual as opposed to artificial needs, Thoreau argues, releases one from the burdens of unnecessary labor in order to pursue worthier goals, meaning for him especially the pleasures of mind-expanding contemplation and deepening immersion in his natural surroundings. This prepares the way for the following chapter, "Where I Lived and What I Lived For," which redescribes that inner and more essential quest to "front the essential facts of life" and penetrate "through the mud and slush of opinion" to a bedrock sense of reality. "Be it life or death, we crave only reality," he sums up—in a characteristic mix of hyperbolic exuberance, teeth-gritting determination, and freakish drollery. "If we are really dying, let us hear the rattle in our throats and feel cold in the extremities; if we are alive, let us go about our business."[3]

"Civil Disobedience" likewise advocates reducing government to the minimum by pushing to the limit the spirit of democratic devolution. Government should confine itself to functions that promote the welfare of its citizens and should otherwise leave them alone. Although Thoreau says little here about the virtues of thrift

and downscaling, he describes the lifestyle conducive to civil disobedience in similar terms. A person with few material possessions
and social entanglements is best positioned to act on conscience.
Here too, then, a nonmaterialistic voluntary simplicity is seen as key
to unlocking one's worthier impulses. *Walden's* assertion that "My
greatest skill has been to want for little" holds for the Thoreauvian
civil disobedient as well.[4]

These affinities also expose the ambiguities and the limits of
Thoreau's radicalism. It risks self-contradiction by appealing to
opposite myths of history. In "Civil Disobedience" Thoreau seems a
child of the Enlightenment in arguing for the completion of democratic revolution against top-down government. Even though he
warns in no uncertain terms that the goal he seeks is nowhere in
sight, his general line of argument appeals to an optimistic view of
history as progress toward recognition of "the individual as a higher
and independent power, from which all its own power and authority
are derived."[5] *Walden* will have none of this. It invokes an opposite
vision of allegedly less materialistic and more egalitarian epochs of
preindustrial times, from the Puritan era back to antecedent dispensations of aboriginal hunter-gatherers and Arcadian antiquity.
It heaps scorn on so-called progress, factory-system regimentation,
runaway materialism, and instrumental exploitation of nature, and
offers scant hope for positive systemic change. Taken together, then,
the two works offer a provocative contrast between Thoreau as a
modernizer in the sphere of political theory but an antimodernizer
in his asperity toward the material fruits of modernization that were
part and parcel of the bourgeois revolution that originally brought
the rights of man to the fore.

The underlying difference here is admittedly less than I have
made it seem. The disparate visions of history are invoked to the
common end of underscoring the threat of soul-killing herd-think.
That in turn, however, exposes the much more problematic issue of
the limits of Thoreau's iconoclasm itself in directing its energies so

exclusively toward liberation of the individual from the constraints of the group.

As Thoreau partly sensed but did not fully realize, his faith in the possibility of transformation at the individual level presupposed a freedom of action that came most readily to persons of relative privilege and security like himself, backstopped by family, friends, and mentors. Nor did he grasp the extent to which he himself was an artifact of the provincial ethos he saw himself opposing, a fellow inheritor of a culture that prized moral backbone and economic self-sufficiency, at least in principle. Thoreauvian voluntary simplicity drew on a dimension of Protestant reform thinking at least two centuries old. His theory of economy was in that sense mainstream, his antimaterialism a ready-to-hand club that had been brandished for generations by the pious against the greedy. From that standpoint, his critique of the work ethic was less a rejection of cultural norms than an insider dispute about what qualifies as a worthy calling.

Furthermore: for how many of Thoreau's contemporaries was it literally true that they came face-to-face with state authority only once a year, as "Civil Disobedience" claims? Certainly not the socially precarious, probably not even most of his Yankee audience, nor himself either. What counts here, however, is not so much strict accuracy as the telltale sense of prevailing insulation from the long arm of the law. Confidence in one's self-sufficiency can also provoke intolerance of slackness in others. So too with Thoreau. Lack of punctuality irked him to the point of imagining the delinquent party begrimed by dirt. Running through his work are putdowns of the indiscipline or inefficiency of non-Yankees: Native Americans, French Catholics, Irish immigrants like the family encountered halfway through *Walden* to whose patriarch our hero vainly preaches his gospel of economy ("The culture of an Irishman is an enterprise to be undertaken with a sort of moral bog hoe"). At times, the mantras of self-sufficiency can sound downright callous, as when *Walden* indicts philanthropy as "goodness tainted," at best a distraction from the pursuit of self-fashioning, at worst a symptom of the reformer's emotional neediness.[6]

Such judgmentalism has understandably drawn sharp criticism of Thoreau's alleged self-focus, insensitivity, and racism. Defenders have responded by citing such extenuating factors as the faddishness of philanthropy in Thoreau's day, his proven record of cordial relations with Irish neighbors, his assistance to fugitive slaves, and his increasing efforts over time to come to terms with Native cultures as living cultures. Overall, the precise extent to which Thoreau's ethics of personal liberation was blinkered by culture, class, and ideology is likely to remain forever unresolved, insofar as it reflects the judgment calls posterity must make of all historical actors with the awakening of public consciousness over time to once-dominant forms of moral blindness: Shall we judge the person as a vessel half empty or half full? Meanwhile, having mapped the basic contours and limits of Thoreau's ethics of liberation, we stand to gain a more nuanced sense of it when we appreciate how it meant more to him than a set of fixed ideas.

Thoreau's sententiousness creates a trap for unwary readers. "Money is not required to buy one necessary of the soul"; "If you have any enterprise before you, try it in your old clothes"; "If I knew for a certainty that a man was coming to my house with the conscious intention of doing me good, I should run for my life"; "The civilized man is a more experienced and wiser savage"; "There is not one of my readers who has yet lived a whole human life"—the cascade of pontifications suggests dogmatic certainty.[7] A closer look reveals a more complicated scene. Only the first and last are offered as literal truth, and their tones are quite different, the one earnest and the other a deadpan wisecrack. The second and third are deliberate hyperboles. The fourth can be understood only if one grasps that "civilized" and "savage" are not the antonyms they are usually taken to be. Driving whatever point at hand is a restless shape-shifting energy, by turns earnest, ironic, whimsical, theatrical. Yes, Thoreau was an irrepressible moralizer, but with a wry awareness of his penchant for crotchety overkill; of the self-contradiction of presuming that others should follow his own life-scripts; and of the incongruity of his own backslidings from the preachments of his monitorial self, which at times he blithely ignores.

In a typical Thoreau discourse, straight-faced position-taking is infused with histrionic elements ranging from over-the-top brio to self-parody. The epigraph on *Walden*'s title page forewarns the reader. It is taken from the chapter that comes closest to summing up the personal stakes of his experiment: "I do not propose to write an ode to dejection, but to brag as lustily as chanticleer in the morning, standing on his roost, if only to wake my neighbors up." High seriousness and parody get crunched together here: the crowing rooster as a symbol of Revelation in Christian iconography and Chanticleer the strutting braggart in Chaucer's Canterbury tale, with a swipe at Coleridgean romantic melancholy along the way. So too with the Thoreau who presents himself valiantly hacking down the weeds of his beanfield as Achilles slew Hector, then confessing negligence and dereliction, even professing indifference (or is it mock indifference?) as to whether or not his crop failed. Then there is the Thoreau who stands bemusedly and unrepentantly apart from his own prescriptions, the Thoreau who slyly observes that his spartan food regimen is offered "rather from an economic than a dietetic point of view," and the reader should not "put my abstemiousness to the test unless he has a well-stocked larder."[8]

Out of this mix a more intimate voice begins to emerge from the sententious one. For some, the mingling of the two may inspire a sense of kinship with the imagined author as fellow traveler, as if Thoreau were beckoning especially to them like e. e. cummings in the "Introduction" to his 1938 *Collected Poems*: these poems "are for you and for me and are not for mostpeople."[9] This feeling of special kinship can overtake the most sophisticated readers, like a former colleague of mine, a political philosopher with a passion for the outdoors, who was certain that he and Thoreau would have gotten along famously had they met in life notwithstanding Thoreau's notorious skittishness. Nor am I the only Thoreau scholar originally drawn to his work partly by that special sense of rapport who has found it necessary in later years to correct against overconfidence in my intuitive sense of who the real Thoreau was.

The most explicit way that Thoreau tempers dogmatism while maintaining his core convictions is by warning against imitation. His disclaimer that civil disobedience is not for everybody does so with particular emphasis. "They who know of no purer sources of truth," he grants, "stand, and wisely stand, by the Bible and the Constitution." Indeed, he goes much further than issuing a mere waiver of obligation to take the nobler path. He insists that the path itself is conditional, not final: "my position, as present," a position that may change. Ultimately a person must "see that he does only what belongs to himself and to the hour."[10]

Walden seems even more emphatically committed to the path of voluntary simplicity as antidote for the discontented. But the disclaimer after making his case is even more sweeping: "I would not have any one adopt *my* mode of living on any account," first, because "before he has fairly learned it I may have found out another for myself," and moreover, "I would have each one be very careful to find out and pursue *his own* way."[11]

Through such fusion of advocacy and qualification, *Walden*, "Civil Disobedience," and Thoreau's writing generally transmit a sense of strongly held and experientially tested principles in the awareness that convictions worthy of the name are independently derived judgments always in process. This flexibility is reinforced by the playful self-reflexiveness under the didactic veil.

Among major essayists in Western literature since classical times, Thoreau was hardly unique in seasoning earnestness with witty byplay. The high seriousness of Seneca, Bacon, and Ruskin is no more typical than Montaigne's wryly self-effacing relativism, Emerson's skeptical bemusement, and the convoluted ironies of Carlyle. Most latter-day writers influenced by Thoreau show analogous mixtures of earnestness and wit: John Muir, Aldo Leopold,

E. B. White, Edward Abbey, even Rachel Carson. Where Thoreau stands out more distinctly is the extent to which he presents himself as wholehearted advocate-enactor of his moral models while insisting on their experimental character. The fusion of passion and provisionality helps explain the enormous range of neo-Thoreauvian ventures that have laid claim to his mantle, from the quick getaway kind to drastic permanent retrenchments; and the ideological and tactical differences among those inspired by his opposition to the political and social orders of his day, from right to left, from notional dissent to extreme self-sacrifice.

Do such divergent outcomes suggest a Thoreau at odds with himself? He himself courts that impression when what seems offered as absolute truth is abruptly recast as nonbinding. Yet probably he would have seen no inherent contradiction between the penchant for moral certainty and the insistence on the tentativeness of any attempt at realization. For a writer convinced that one's genius is one's proper guide to distance himself from the stance of certainty when that mood gave way to second thoughts was only fitting.

"Civil Disobedience" and *Walden* both evoke a vivid sense of biographical incident but remain cagey on details. "Civil Disobedience" never explains why Thoreau stopped paying taxes well before the Mexican War, the nominal trigger. *Walden* is vague about why the author began his experiment when he did and why. Scholars continue to puzzle over whether his removal to Walden was more likely prompted by a desire for private space for concentrated writing, a reaction to feeling socially marginalized, or a more general sense of life impasse or vocational crossroads. Thoreau encourages such guesswork with cryptic allusions to past enterprises and disappointments and hints that Walden is a good place to conduct business without ever disclosing the specifics of his decision, the timing, or the projects to which he alludes.

To keep the backstories of "Civil Disobedience" and *Walden* rather generic had the obvious advantages, however, of allowing readers to fit his lifeline to theirs and reinforcing what he himself had come to believe, that the autobiographical experiences on which both works were based were not merely idiosyncratic but exemplary, paradigmatic.

Tax resistance must not have been the first illegal act Thoreau ever contemplated, for he had been meditating off and on about conflicts between law and conscience since his college years. But it was his first overt defiance of the law's authority. "Resistance to Civil Government," as he titled the first printed version of his lecture-essay, was commensurately more assertive than his previous, much more desultory and ambivalent "reform" pieces, which commend perpetual readiness for brave action and chide the quixotic overreach of utopian social reengineering and the emotional overheatedness of reform culture. His nearest approach to "Civil Disobedience" had been an 1841 Concord Lyceum debate in which his brother and he took the affirmative side of the question "Is It Ever Proper to Offer Resistance?"—ironically in opposition to fellow Transcendentalist Bronson Alcott, later one of his own models. But that was still just talk. "Civil Disobedience" was the defense of an actual act that embodied the theory that became the cornerstone of his political thought.

Thoreau's relocation to Walden prepared the way for both act and essay as a public enactment of social outsidership. That move was even more deeply premeditated and even more permanently consequential. Indeed, it was the most momentous turning point in his mental life, the belated realization of a long dream, which he never ceased to regard as a formative experience, especially during the half-dozen years he continued work on the book after the sojourn ended.

Significantly, *Walden* describes his removal not only as a fresh start but as a symbolic return, to one of the "oldest scenes stamped on my memory," of being taken as a four-year-old "from Boston to this my native town, through these very woods and this field, to the pond."[12] The longer journal passage from which this comes describes the memory of "that woodland vision" as "the oriental asiatic valley of my world," which "for a long time made the drapery of my dreams. . . . Somehow or other it at once gave the preference to this recess among the pines," as if his spirit "had found its proper nursery." That Thoreau's juvenescent hankerings from age four returned him to the pond at age twenty-eight was partly fortuitous, of course. It might not have happened unless Emerson had bought the woodlot where he roosted. But the enactment seemed a consummation nonetheless. "The thought of Walden in the woods yonder" runs through his early *Journal*: the hankering to live by the pond and listen to the "wind whispering among the trees" and "watch the progress of the seasons."[13] Nor did he leave the pond behind when he left it. One telltale sign is *Walden*'s deliberate confusion of tenses: the mingling of past, present, and habitual or ongoing time, as if the action were happening even as the speaker relates it. The common image of Thoreau as a denizen of the woods who never really returned home is broadly true to his inner life if not his outer.

After leaving Walden, Thoreau continued to research its history for years through town archives, local testimony, and folklore. For the rest of his life, he would return there thousands of times in body or in dream. On the daily walks into which he settled in the late 1840s, Walden was a favored stop. He never ceased to savor its vistas; the pleasures of boating and swimming; the zest for tracking such environmental fluctuations as the pond's rise and fall, freeze and thaw, the elegiac contemplation of the ongoing deforestation of its shores; the slow decay of his beanfield and the fate of his house, eventually sold to a local farmer.

The rethinking, rewriting, and additions prompted by these aftermaths were crucial to the descriptive and philosophic nuances of the finished book, especially the dramatization of the pond as an active agent, the mix of exuberant affirmation and nostalgic wistfulness, and the sense of his own experiment as embedded in the flow of natural and historical time.

Another mark of Thoreau's long investment in his subject— much the same holds for "Civil Disobedience" too—is the pungent sentence-by-sentence intricacy of extended sallies that push a point to its uttermost limits. One from *Walden*'s "Conclusion" sums up the underlying spirit of this rhetoric:

> I fear chiefly lest my expression may not be *extra- vagant* enough, may not wander far enough beyond the narrow limits of my daily experience, so as to be adequate to the truth of which I have been convinced. *Extra vagance!* It depends on how you are yarded. The migrating buffalo, which seeks new pastures in another latitude, is not extravagant like the cow which kicks over the pail, leaps the cow-yard fence, and runs after her calf, in milking time. I desire to speak somewhere *without* bounds: like a man in a waking moment, to men in their waking moments; for I am convinced that I can not exaggerate enough even to lay the foundation of a true expression. Who that has heard a strain of music feared then lest he should speak extravagantly any more forever? In view of the future or possible, we should live quite laxly and undefined in front, our outlines dim and misty on that side; as our shadows reveal an insensible perspiration toward the sun. The volatile truth of our words should continually betray the inadequacy of the residual statement. Their truth is instantly *translated*; its literal monument alone remains.[14]

The passage has the feel of having been pondered a long time in various moods, from the homely to the exalted, from droll and banal barnyard melodrama to the arcane metaphor of perspiring shadows. All this not to force a final formulation, but to provoke the reader to carry forward the work of implementing the spirit of what perforce must remain nothing more than a "residual statement," since as words in a book about a past experience it is only a "monument," not an action.

The durability of *Walden* and "Civil Disobedience," however, has hinged less on individual sallies than on Thoreau's recasting of broader traditions of thought and feeling made fresh and memorable by his articulation of them. The defining template for "Civil

Disobedience" is of course the confrontation between the embattled person of conscience and state injustice, which dates back in Western imagination to Antigone versus Creon in Sophocles. A few years before, Thoreau had identified a partial equivalent in the bravery with which Walter Raleigh faced his execution, and a decade afterward he would praise the martyrdom of John Brown as an example par excellence. "Civil Disobedience" stands out, however, as his one concentrated effort to cast himself as an Antigone. The key to its staying power was its dramatization of the starkest imaginable kind of self-contradiction of values for a nation founded on democratic principles: the antithesis between the claims of individual freedom and legalized chattel slavery.

Walden introduces this same paradigm but draws more heavily on several others. One is do-it-yourself-ism, both in its Yankee-tribal guise of the protagonist as jack of all trades and in its more broadly American-mythic guise of pioneer-style homesteading. Cultural history has shown that the appeal of both also extends well beyond the United States. Thoreau's articulation of it was well timed to capitalize on the burgeoning national iconography of frontiering as well as defensive anxiety about the erosion of independent self-sufficiency with migration from small farms to metropolitan areas and increasingly specialized division of labor under industrialization. The lowly dwellings of the national hinterland had become familiar props of national politics, from the so-called Log Cabin and Hard Cider presidential campaign of 1840, when the venerable frontier warhorse William Henry Harrison defeated the New York machine politician Martin Van Buren; and the growing popularity of what later became nicknamed the American Dream of upward mobility from humble origins, which Thoreau hijacks in the service of his antimaterialist counterdream.

Another symptom of ambivalence to urbanization was the dream of rural retreat that pervaded international Romanticism from Wordsworth's poetry to the rising vogue of rustic suburban cottages. Thoreau evokes its charisma in alluring descriptions of his natural surroundings, the construction of his simple "house" (which he never calls a "cabin"), and the comforts of dwelling in the woods—starting with the frontispiece to the 1854 edition based on his sister Sophia Thoreau's fanciful but enticing sketch.

Walden's admirers were also quick to respond to its loftier and more anciently rooted evocations of contemplative retreat. The author presents himself as devotee and heir of ancient sages: Confucius, Mencius, figures of Indic scripture and classical Persian poetry. Although he insists that he is not a hermit by dis-position, he winds up calling himself one. Though it would have been truer to the impressive amount of writing he did there to call Thoreau's abode a studio, his friend Ellery Channing was not merely fantasizing when he celebrated it as "a little Hermitage, where with much piety he passes life."[15] That captured the sense of exaltation Thoreau felt upon moving to Walden, of being elevated to a higher plane of being, and the idealism that surfaces especially in *Walden's* great credo chapters: "Where I Lived and What I Lived for," "Higher Laws," and "Conclusion." Composed while Thoreau still lived there, Channing's poem "Walden" was history's first shot at memorializing him as the latter-day secular saint or sage or life-guide that he has since become for many.

The most pervasive constituent of rural retirement imagina-tion from antiquity to the present, however, has been centered-ness in place, typically an out-of-the-way place threatened by the invasion of so-called progress. Often, as in *Walden*, the protagonist assumes the role of genius loci or self-appointed guardian. The enduring appeal of such imagined places despite or rather because the tide of modernization has rendered them increasingly obsolete is another reason for *Walden's* iconic durability, to some the most crucial. Its proto-environmentalist charisma has made it the most seminal work of place imagination in Anglophone environmen-tal literature. John Muir's calls for preservation of the American West and Anglo-Argentine naturalist W. H. Hudson's evocations of Patagonia; the literary naturalism of the young Rachel Carson;

WALDEN;

OR,

LIFE IN THE WOODS.

By HENRY D. THOREAU,

AUTHOR OF "A WEEK ON THE CONCORD AND MERRIMACK RIVERS."

I do not propose to write an ode to dejection, but to brag as lustily as chanticleer in the morning, standing on his roost, if only to wake my neighbors up. — Page 92.

BOSTON:
TICKNOR AND FIELDS.
M DCCC LIV.

The title page of *Walden*'s first edition features a romanticized sketch of Thoreau's house, based on a drawing by his younger sister Sophia. A more accurate replica of the house overlooks the east end of Walden Pond by the state reservation parking lot. *Courtesy of the Walden Woods Project.*

Sophia Thoreau, Thoreau's younger sister, shared her brother's botanical interests and his love of music and accompanied him on some of his outings. She became his primary caregiver during his last illness and served as his first literary executor. *By permission of the Concord Museum.*

such classics of twentieth-century nature writing as Edward Abbey's *Desert Solitaire*, Annie Dillard's *Pilgrim at Tinker Creek*, and Barry Lopez's *Arctic Dreams*; the personal-polemical essays of conservation biologists from Aldo Leopold to E. O. Wilson—for all these and many more, *Walden* stands as a perennially cited benchmark if not a direct influence.

Although "Civil Disobedience" and *Walden* were Thoreau's most outstanding embodiments of the templates just surveyed, his deployment of them evolved over the course of his career. "Civil Disobedience" was the cornerstone of his political philosophy, but not its end point. *Walden* proved a stage in the progress of his environmental education and the art and thought to which it led.

Chapter 3

Contexts

Antebellum America, Transcendentalism, Emerson

Thoreau's short life span of forty-four years saw many more far-reaching changes in the fabric of American society than did the previous four decades of independence. At his birth shortly after the War of 1812, the country was a loose conglomeration of nineteen states east of the Mississippi with vast hinterlands unsettled. Compared to Britain and France, it was a minor power underdeveloped economically, militarily, and culturally. Transportation networks were too scanty to bridge its distances. Few so-called cities were larger than today's midsize towns. Literature and the arts relied heavily on imports. Industrial revolution had just begun. Economic and political power was largely controlled by regional white elites, overwhelmingly Anglo-Protestant. By Thoreau's adolescence, all this had begun to change rapidly.

By the time of his death, early in the American Civil War, the northern states were well on the way to transforming the country into a transcontinental industrial superpower. Canals, steam power, railroads, and telegraphy had shrunk distances to a fraction of what they had been. Newspaper, magazine, and book publishing were thriving. Such American literary figures as Irving, Cooper, Longfellow, Emerson, Hawthorne, Harriet Beecher Stowe, and others became increasingly respected and influential both at home and abroad. Agriculture remained the largest economic sector, employing slightly more than half the workforce, but clearly not for long. Northern cities were mushrooming, with the New York / Brooklyn metropolis approaching the size of Paris, the world's third largest city after London and Beijing.

These shifts both followed from and accelerated an unprecedented destabilization of social certitudes a mid-twentieth-century historian nicknamed "freedom's ferment"—an explosion of progressive reform energies and counterreactions.[1] Voting rights, once limited to property-holding males, were extended to all white men, which in turn energized women's rights and antislavery movements but also slaveholder defensiveness. Annexation of Mexico's northern half and immigration from Ireland, Germany, French Canada, Scandinavia, China, and elsewhere diversified the population, especially in the North and West, while hardening and complicating divisions of race and caste. Protestantism split into a welter of disparate sects from neo-Calvinist to atheist, reflecting opposite pressures of revivalism and secularization. Social reform movements proliferated across the North: pacificism; temperance; progressive education; urban sanitation; charities on behalf of the distressed in every sphere—the poor, the imprisoned, the blind, the deaf, the mentally ill. One of the most distinctive developments was an upsurge, unrivaled in US history before or since, of visionary communitarian experiments, both secular and religious: Fourierist, Owenite, Millenarian. Most were short-lived, but a few, like the Latter-Day Saints, became major institutions.

Thoreau's Concord was an incubator, testing ground, and epicenter for many of these energies as the de facto headquarters of one of the defining intellectual movements of the era: American Transcendentalism, whose high point from the mid-1830s to the mid-1840s coincided with his own coming of age.

Transcendentalism's nucleus consisted of several dozen loosely networked women and men born mostly during the early 1800s within a hundred miles of Boston. Few were affluent, but most were from genteel New England stock, and unusually well educated for their time, the men mostly Harvard alumni and many of the women classically educated too. Most were liberal Protestant ministers, teachers of progressive bent, or aspiring writers of poetry or intellectual prose—often some combination of the three.

The Transcendentalists were thinkers and doers rather than institution-builders. Their organized collective efforts were few: several discussion groups, chief among them the "Transcendental Club," which met irregularly for a half-dozen years starting in the mid-1830s; several short-lived intellectual magazines, the most prominent being *The Dial: A Magazine of Literature, Philosophy, and Religion* (1840–44), edited first by Margaret Fuller and then by Ralph Waldo Emerson; and two communes outside Boston, Brook Farm (1841–47) and Fruitlands (1843). That barely added up to a united front. Yet the participants, working autonomously for the most part but cross-pollinating and sometimes collaborating over time, had an outsized impact on the course of literature, religion, philosophy, and social reform thinking.

Their most catalytic figure was Ralph Waldo Emerson, who was also the reason for Concord's centrality. Scion of a line of Congregational ministers dating back two centuries to the early Puritans, Emerson resigned his pastorate at a prominent Boston church in his late twenties and removed to the ancestral home of the Emersons during Thoreau's college years. Thanks to an inheritance from his first wife's estate and the graciousness of his second, he made his spacious house a salon of sorts and blossomed into a freelance lecturer, essayist, and poet of international fame, becoming eventually the nation's foremost public intellectual. His career bore out the verdict of the movement's first historian, O. B. Frothingham, that Transcendentalism started as a religious ferment but was "essentially poetical" and expressed itself most characteristically in literary form.[2]

At the center of the Transcendentalist centrifuge was a broadly shared conviction in "the infinitude of the private man," to quote

Emerson's encapsulation of the "one doctrine" at the heart of his work.[3] Human infinitude proved an intense and adaptable burning lens for incinerating orthodoxies on multiple fronts. In religion, Emerson and his colleagues invoked it to press the claims of individual spiritual intuition against the authority of scripture, doctrine, and church. In literature and the arts, they used it to assert the superiority of genius to craftsmanship and discredit neoclassical formalism. In social thought, they assailed the factitiousness of status and male privilege, the inhumanity of slavery, and the scandal of widening economic inequality. In education, they discredited the authority of top-down pedagogy and the fetishization of drill. In philosophy, they advanced the claims of Reason or higher intuition over Understanding, or rational empiricism.

In approaching all these subjects, the Transcendentalists started from the assumption of a universal human nature, in terms of which differences of culture, gender, race, and region seemed diffracting prisms that offered distinctive pathways but at the same time interposed barriers to full actualization of the ideal. This cosmopolitanism served well for discrediting provincial elitisms—post-Puritan dogmatism, Yankee jingoism, Brahmin complacency—and for advancing counterclaims for the comparative legitimacy of non-Western religions and the power of aspiration to offset disadvantages of race, gender, and social position. It also blinded the Transcendentalists to the recalcitrance of those barriers and to their own provincialisms, such as the ideology of autonomous spiritual bootstrapping at the heart of the Emersonian vision. In this, they resembled the Enlightenment philosophes before them and those advocates of the Universal Declaration of Human Rights a century later who failed to reckon with dismissals of their version of human rights as a Eurocentric imposition.

The vision of human infinitude was nonetheless well timed to inspire a restless younger generation of progressive northern white youth growing up at the moment when the last of the nation's founders were passing away, when Romanticism was jumping the Atlantic, when German so-called Higher Criticism of the Bible was exposing it as humanly constructed rather than divinely inspired, when the extension of voting rights to unpropertied white males was upending American political culture, when Britain was enacting electoral reform at home and abolishing slavery in its Caribbean colonies, and when the antislavery and women's rights movements in the United States were beginning to surge. Coming when it did, in the form it did, Transcendentalism thereby became American history's first intellectual vanguard to advance the claims of youthful energy and insight over the wisdom of age. To imagine the United States as a young nation was nothing new—standard doctrine since the Revolutionary era. But the national tradition of countercultural movements on youth's behalf starts here.

Emerson spread the gospel in inspirational "lay sermons," as he liked to call them, typically delivered first as public lectures and then distilled into lapidary prose. Some of his best were unveiled just as Thoreau came of age: his 1836 *Nature* ("Why should not we also enjoy an original relation to the universe?"); "The American Scholar," his 1837 challenge to conventional academic rigor (books "are for nothing but to inspire"); his fiery address to the Divinity School class of 1838 ("Yourself a newborn bard of the Holy Ghost, cast behind you all conformity, and acquaint men at first hand with Deity"); and "Self-Reliance," the centerpiece of his 1841 *Essays, First Series* ("Trust thyself: every heart vibrates to that iron string").[4] He availed himself masterfully of the burgeoning new Lyceum system, a network of town-based adult education and entertainment forums that spread throughout the North during the second quarter of the nineteenth century.

Other prominent Transcendentalists included Margaret Fuller, Bronson Alcott, Elizabeth Peabody, George Ripley, Orestes Brownson, and Theodore Parker. Alcott was a self-taught schoolteacher-philosopher who joined Emerson in Concord after the collapse of his experimental Boston school, founded on the inherent divinity of the child. Peabody, his polymathic assistant and an educational thinker in her own right, went on to start a bookstore and publishing business that became a Transcendentalist hub. Fuller worked briefly with Alcott, served a while as Emerson's editorial colleague, semi-intimate, and sparring partner. She then became the Transcendentalists' leading advocate for women's rights with the first American feminist manifesto, *Woman in the Nineteenth Century*, which she completed after embarking on a journalistic career that took her first to New York and then to Europe as reporter of and partisan in the Italian Revolution of 1848. Ripley, Brownson, and Parker were Unitarian clergymen who followed discrepant paths. Parker became Transcendentalism's most erudite and combative theologian, and an eloquent preacher whose vehement abolitionism and advocacy for the urban poor helped inspire the Social Gospel movement later in the century. Ripley left the ministry to found Brook Farm with his wife, Sophia, and when it folded he joined Fuller on the staff of what was then the country's one newspaper with anything like nationwide circulation, the *New York Tribune:* she its celebrity foreign correspondent, he its lead book reviewer. The disputatious Brownson scrolled through a series of pastorates, becoming for a time a prodigiously prolific reform journalist and America's first Marxist critic of economic injustice. At midlife, he abruptly converted to Catholicism and became an unsparing foe of the movement he had helped to launch.

Thoreau knew all six, some intimately. All took part in Transcendental Club meetings, which he joined at Emerson's invitation at about its midpoint. Afterward, he kept in touch with them all at least intermittently. Brownson became, briefly, his first intellectual mentor, when Thoreau boarded with him as a resident-tutee on leave from Harvard. With the gentler Alcott, nearly twenty years his senior, he formed a lifelong intimacy. They were drawn to each other as conversation partners receptive to each other's wildest speculations and as kindred outliers even fellow Transcendentalists thought eccentric. Fuller became an early confidant despite roundly criticizing his early *Dial* submissions. She may have been the first person with whom he shared the dream of homesteading at Walden. Altogether, Thoreau was the nearest of all the movement's major figures to having been born Transcendental: its only birthright Concordian and the scion with the greatest number of significant elders. His closest companion of the same age other than his siblings was still another Transcendentalist: Ellery Channing, the movement's most prolific poet, Thoreau's most frequent walking partner, and later his first biographer.

None was so important to Thoreau as Emerson, however. Indeed, the Emerson-Thoreau relation has few if any parallels in world history. Rarely has the disciple of so seminal a figure risen to equal or greater prominence in his own right. For this to have happened when the disciple spent his entire life in such proximity to the master is truly extraordinary.

Their first recorded meeting took place in 1837, when Thoreau was fresh from college and Emerson already a rising star. For Thoreau, it inspired the momentous decision to start the journal he kept for the rest of his life. (" 'What are you doing now?' he asked? 'Do you keep a journal?'—So I make my first entry today.")[5] Emerson, for his part, was impressed by the bright young iconoclast. Always on the lookout for youthful promise, he seized on Thoreau as his first local recruit. Over the next dozen years, he encouraged Thoreau's ambitions, drawing him into his intellectual circle, soliciting contributions for the *Dial*, reading drafts, lobbying publishers. Thoreau even spent two years in the early 1840s living at the Emersons', as a resident handyman, tutor, editorial assistant, and interlocutor. After that, Emerson arranged a post for him as tutor to the children of his New York lawyer-brother to give him a shot at literary Manhattan. After his 1845–47 sojourn at Walden Pond—on Emerson's land— he spent another lengthy stint at the Emersons' as household head in the patriarch's absence on a foreign lecture tour. Later their relationship cooled, but their paths continued to cross frequently, Emerson never ceasing to keep a watchful eye on his balky ex-pupil despite Thoreau's resentment at what seemed Emerson's condescending urbanity as he became a household word and Thoreau remained in provincial obscurity.

Ralph Waldo Emerson sat for this portrait in 1854, when he was the leading public intellectual in the antebellum North. Emerson was much more photographed than Thoreau, his obscure mentee. According to Emerson's son Edward, this was the image his father liked best. It shows him in his prime. Photograph by Josiah Johnson Hawes from a daguerreotype taken in 1856. *National Portrait Gallery.*

Emerson became somewhat disenchanted as well. When Thoreau proved a slow producer, Emerson began to think of him as a case of early promise unfulfilled. This was actually a typical Emerson syndrome, as Walt Whitman and other protégés were to find: initial excitement giving way to critical second thoughts. Emerson's curious address at Thoreau's funeral is in keeping. Apart from the appendix of select Thoreau sayings, it says little about his work except to lament the unnamed "broken task which none can finish" that Thoreau left undone at his early death and to chide him for lack of ambition. ("Instead of engineering for all America," he was content to be "the captain of a huckleberry party," Emerson complains, in a backhanded allusion to "Civil Disobedience.")[6] After such reservations, Emerson's closing insistence that Thoreau's death was a grievous loss to the nation sounds like wishful thinking. Altogether, his "Thoreau" ensured that the then-prevalent image of Thoreau as Emerson's cranky sidekick would persist well into the twentieth century, as well-meaning publishers drew on it repeatedly for advertising material and as preface to editions of Thoreau's work.

In fact, Emerson never ceased to admire Thoreau's integrity, quickness of thought, and cornucopia of practical talents, on which he greatly relied, enlisting Thoreau not only as gardener and handyman and playmate for his children but also as surrogate household head and literary executor with carte blanche to correct proofs. He remained very fond of Thoreau personally too, as did the whole Emerson family, a fact his son Edward Emerson confirmed in his affectionate memoir, *Henry Thoreau as Remembered by a Young Friend* (1917). Even Thoreau's prickliness struck Emerson as more piquant than offensive. Thoreau kept him on his toes. Beyond his practical wizardry in areas where Emerson was clueless, Thoreau was not only incomparably the better naturalist; he also had a far more acutely discriminating ear and painterly eye; and his grasp of languages, cultures, and history rivaled Emerson's and in a number of areas surpassed it.

Emerson's second wife, Lidian Emerson, holds toddler Edward. Lidian was the woman to whom Thoreau felt closest other than his mother and sisters. Edward, the youngest of her four children, looked on Thoreau as a father-figure as well as playmate. *Courtesy of the Concord Free Public Library.*

If little of this history surfaces in Emerson's address, Transcendentalism itself is partly to blame. The loftiness with which he weighs Thoreau's qualities in the balance resembles the magisterial tone he struck when sizing up the famous figures of history: Plato, Shakespeare, Montaigne, Napoleon, Goethe. Such was biography, Transcendentalist style. When human potential is boundless, even the most impressive lives fall short. Had Thoreau outlived Emerson, he might well have eulogized his mentor in a similar vein.

Emerson's coolness also had a more personal dimension. He habitually favored an air of benign reserve, infinitely vexing to more ardent dispositions who tried to penetrate it, including even his second wife Lidian. The sense of confronting a personage rather than a person galled Thoreau increasingly as he entered his thirties hoping for a greater reciprocity. Tellingly, only once, and then only with extreme self-consciousness in a letter sent across the Atlantic, is Thoreau known to have addressed Emerson as "Waldo." Even in his journal, it was always "Emerson" or "Mr. Emerson." It did not help matters that Thoreau himself was stiffish and defensive. Small-town classism was another aggravation: Emerson was pedigreed local gentry, he the son of a small entrepreneur and a boardinghouse keeper.

On the upside, such tensions helped detach disciple from mentor. Significantly, the common first impression that Thoreau was a copycat version of Emerson, down to mannerisms of voice and gesture, tended to fade on closer acquaintance. So too with their writings. Their genres, styles, and methods of composition were similar. Both were best at sententious intellectual prose, as poets hit or miss, and zealous keepers of journals, from which they distilled their essays, often with lectures as trial runs. Many of Emerson's hallmark topics anticipate Thoreau's: Nature, Self-Reliance, Experience, Heroism, Higher Laws, Politics, Reform. Often we find Thoreau revising or inverting Emerson, sometimes down to the minutest capillaries. "Civil Disobedience" cherry-picks the more radical thrusts from Emerson's "Politics" and runs with them: "the less government we have, the better," "Good men must not obey the laws too well."[7]

Thoreau's "Be it life or death, we crave only reality" answers back to a despairing passage in Emerson's "Experience."[8] *Walden*'s long chapter "Economy," whether or not so intended, undermines the zest for material progress with which Emerson treats the subject of "Commodity" in *Nature*.

Not that Thoreau composed with Emerson's books by his side. *Essays, Second Series* (1844), the third of the eight volumes Emerson published during Thoreau's lifetime, was probably the last he read more than skimmingly. The lion's share of his mature writing came well after his immersion in Emerson's. That was why it became not merely an extension of it but an increasingly independent swerve.

To understand how Transcendentalism served as a launching pad that enabled Thoreau's reach to surpass Emerson's, consider Thoreau's engagement with two preeminent idols of the Transcendentalist tribe: reverence for nature and for unlimited human potential. In each case, Thoreau gave lasting embodiment to a sketchy model and recast it so distinctively that his versions became the seminal exempla.

Transcendentalist assertions of human divinity were long on dream but short on implementation. "The mission of this Age," Alcott insisted, was "to reproduce Perfect Men,"[9] but his exempla were confined to anecdotes of schoolchildren coaxed to express their higher promptings. Emerson offered general recipes for self-transformation via contemplation of nature and resistance of conventional expectation. Parker repeatedly affirmed that "the great truths of morality and religion" are accessed "intuitively, and by instinct," not by theology; but when he descended to detail, he concentrated on itemizing the abuses of the latter rather than the promise of the former.[10] Brownson urged grand schemes for uplifting humanity by demolition and reconstruction of the whole socioeconomic order. Thoreau alone gave this ambient enthusiasm memorable concrete embodiment in "Civil Disobedience" and especially in *Walden*. Thanks largely to their influence, Emerson has become remembered as the prophet of Self-Reliance and Thoreau as the one who enacted it. Their supposed exchange at Thoreau's prison window—Why are you in there? Why aren't you in here with me?—has become a canonical fable although it has no basis in fact.[11] The gusto with which *Walden* unpacks its ethics of self-sufficient simplicity and the work of house-building seems at once a robust response to *Nature*'s closing call "Build, therefore, your own world" and a reproach to its grandiosity.[12] Indeed, *Walden* stages the movement's most down-to-earth original enactment both of Emerson's vision of self-trust and of *Nature*'s multistep prescription for nature's awakening of a person's higher powers.

The success of Thoreau's work in dramatizing Self-Reliance in action hinged not only on gusto and granularity but also his enlistment of the paradigmatic or exemplary narrative form. Literary Transcendentalism strongly favored essayistic exposition of ideas, with poetry as the preferred medium for more purely creative flights. Except for Thoreau's, the overwhelming majority of Transcendentalist writing was in one or the other vein: Emerson's essays, Fuller's *Woman in the Nineteenth Century* and late journalistic dispatches, Brownson's "The Laboring Classes," Parker's "Transient and Permanent in Christianity"; the best poems of Emerson, Thoreau, Channing, Jones Very, and Ellen Sturgis Hooper. Although the vision of human infinitude implied a bildungsroman-like plotline of personal emergence from inauthenticity to self-realization, apart from *Walden* the nearest approximation to an enduring work of such kind to come out of the movement was Louisa May Alcott's novel *Little Women*, which can be understood as an affectionate-critical rejoinder to both Emerson and Thoreau by a member of the next generation of born-Transcendentals. Like *Walden*, *Little Women* features an exemplary limit-bumping young protagonist, but one who eventually settles, as the author herself did, for something closer to a socially approved compromise with the entanglements she had dreamed of escaping.

Alcott's greater mindfulness of the claims of family and society on the individual, for better or for worse, also alerts us that the image of

Thoreau as the disciple who embodied Emerson-style Self-Reliance theory oversimplifies the trajectories of the Transcendentalist movement as a whole. It wasn't just about individual fulfillment but also about the transformation of society. The communitarian experiments of Bronson Alcott and the Ripleys and the social manifestoes of Brownson and Parker were as symptomatic of the Transcendentalist quest to realize the potential of human infinitude as the emphasis put by Emerson and especially Thoreau on transformation at the individual level. Indeed, this became a recurring bone of contention within the group, as when Emerson and Thoreau flatly refused to join Brook Farm and were chided by some of their colleagues for evasion of social responsibility. The image of polarity is itself simplistic, however. Neither Emerson nor Thoreau saw the value of Self-Reliance as its benefit for the individual person exclusively. It was also the key to broader social transformation, however much they tended to speak of the latter prospect skeptically as a second-order and much less probable goal. Their belated but increasingly earnest participation in antislavery activism confirms this. That too explains some of the tension that developed between them: Thoreau pushing Emerson's newfound political oppositionalism to a further extreme in "Civil Disobedience," Emerson thereupon complaining about the irresponsibility of Thoreau's gesture, Thoreau chastising the worldlier Emerson for evasion of hard facts, Emerson complaining about Thoreau's lack of ambition in his funeral address. In any case, Thoreau has come to stand for posterity as the incarnation of Self-Reliance theory as well as its downsides of willful idiosyncrasy and disregard for society's rightful claims.

Thoreau's engagement with the natural world is an equally dramatic example of drawing from Transcendentalism to become its defining exemplar even as he grew away from it. Up to a point, Transcendentalism supplied the groundwork and tailwind for him to become an inventor of modern nature writing, a pioneer ecologist before the term was coined, and an inspiration for modern environmentalists. Virtually all the Transcendentalists shared a notional

reverence for physical nature in keeping with the Romanticist idealization of nature as an antipode to the dislocating techno-social
changes then underway: urbanization, industrial transformation of
the countryside, and erosion of intergenerational embeddedness
in place by increased mobility and the ideology of perpetual progress. Their idealization of nature was further reinforced by the anti-
supernaturalist version of Protestantism they also broadly shared,
which looked to nature as a locus of the sacred more authentic than
the revelations of scripture. Most were armchair naturalists, however: town or city dwellers by choice if not by birth, whose main
contact with actual nature came in periodic short rambles and whose
evocations of nature tended to be luminously unspecific.

Thoreau's early thought and writing also fits that mold, predictably enough for a townsman's son. But as a youth of practical hands-
on bent who loved the outdoors, who harbored the dream of living
in a self-built cabin by a pond as his freshman roommate had actually
done, he was also disposed to take more literally Emerson's dictum
that a scholar's first resource should be nature rather than books.

Nature celebrates the inspirational effects of human connectedness to the natural world, but its theory of the epistemological
basis of that connectedness remains quite metaphysical. Nature and
humankind are parallel manifestations of Spirit, such that nature
presents itself as a "metaphor of the human mind" whereby the laws
of nature correspond to the laws of ethics and natural phenomena
reveal themselves to the awakened eye as the basis of a vast symbol-
system that forms the proper basis of human thought and expression. Rightly understood, words derive from nature—"spirit" from
"wind," for example—and natural processes are symbolically significant: ripples in a pool into which a stone is cast "are the beautiful
type of all influence."[13]

This theory of the symbolic "correspondence" between natural
and moral worlds, which Emerson derived from medieval and modern mystical sources, was well suited to energize a thinker of poetic,
mystical, and nature-loving disposition, and it had a formative and

long-lasting impact on Thoreau. *Walden*'s conjectures about the symbolic meaning of the pond, its triumphant demonstration of the ethical significance of its geometry, and its depiction of the year's seasonal cycle as a symbol of spiritual renewal are all applications of Emersonian correspondence theory. But as the biology and the material palpability of the natural world became more and more important to Thoreau, he grew away from the theory even as he availed himself of it. *Walden* attests to this shift in its elaboration of the literal biology and geology of the pond and surroundings; in its portrayal of the pond's literal purity and ecology, not just its symbolism; and its evocations of his ongoing interaction with the animal life of the place: sparrows perching on his shoulder, mice feeding from his hands, squirrels running over his feet. All these increasingly figure not merely as observed phenomena, but as part of a material habitat in whose literality the persona comes to immerse himself to such an extent that his insistence toward the close on the human need for "the tonic of wildness" in all its sensuous plenitude seems a logical upshot: to wade in the marshes "where the bittern and the meadow-hen lurk," to "hear the booming of the snipe," to "smell the whispering sedge," and even to relish the spectacle of the rotting carcass of a dead horse in a hollow on the path to town ("I love to see that nature is so rife with life").[14]

The preeminent value Thoreau came to set on sensuous immersion in nature, on understanding of its literal workings, and on defending its integrity from human assault—these were the bases for his later elevation into an icon of Transcendentalism's devotion to nature. All were nurtured by Transcendentalism in the first instance; but they propelled him in a different ethical direction from Emersonian theory. Emerson's *Nature* rests on a view of nature as a resource for humankind—economic, aesthetic, intellectual, spiritual. It rejects at the outset the possibility that humans might seriously imperil the natural order and never considers whether they have an obligation to preserve it. Despite its celebration of the beauty of woods, stars, fields, and streams and the sense of rapport and inspiration contact with them affords, *Nature*'s dominant ethos is instrumental—as consistent with the ideology of aggressive westwarding and techno-economic transformation as with the spirit of the environmentalist movements that formed later in the century. Among the Transcendentalists, Thoreau alone began to move toward a view of nature as a value in and of itself, toward a biocentric reconception of the ethical relation between human and nonhuman.

Altogether, then, to conceive of Thoreau as the exemplar of Transcendentalist thinking about Self-Reliance and of Nature is both anachronistic and fitting. Anachronistic, because the Thoreau chiefly known by posterity had outgrown his original auspices; but fitting because Transcendentalism was the primary intellectual context out of which he grew—and also because Thoreau himself seems to have taken a certain pleasure in reaffirming his affiliation with it, even as the movement began to seem to his contemporaries, including its original fomenters, increasingly bygone.

The movement was on the wane well before *Walden*'s completion, with the collapse of Brook Farm, Fuller's journalistic turn and death in 1850, and Emerson's midcareer shift from fervent idealist to man-of-the-world pragmatist. Many of the group had been restive from the start at the imputation of a united front, and most disliked the Transcendentalist label, much ridiculed by detractors as a synonym for foreign nonsense. (Visiting Boston in 1842, novelist Charles Dickens was told that "whatever was unintelligible would be certainly transcendental.")[15] Hence Emerson tops off a mock-nostalgic late-life memoir of the movement by absurdly claiming that the participants were all "surprised at this rumor of a school or sect, & certainly at the name of Transcendentalism, which nobody knows who gave, or when it was first applied."[16]

Thoreau, by contrast, persisted in calling himself a Transcendentalist for the rest of his life, in full awareness that the term had long since become a synonym for oddball. Why? Partly, it seems, to anticipate and disarm imagined resistance with a bit of whimsical humor. But perhaps such flourishes also implied a sense of having refashioned the movement's original premises according to his own vision. If so, what could have been more Transcendental?

Chapter 4

The Writer

Thoreau looms largest in history as a literary presence, a leading figure in US literary emergence in the mid-nineteenth century, when a critical mass of American authors started publishing creative writing of a level of originality that won international attention.

Like Emerson and Whitman and Melville, Thoreau did not come into his own as a writer until his thirties. One key reason was that authorship as a viable profession then barely existed. Those who hoped to make a living as creative writers almost always had to depend on support from family and friends or on a more reliable income. For the tiny fraction of white college-educated American men, of whom Thoreau was one, the most common choices were the "learned" professions of law, ministry, and medicine, often prefaced by stints of schoolteaching. Thoreau took two stabs at teaching, but after the academy he cofounded with his brother folded when John's health failed, he forsook the standard professional paths, relying thereafter on an eclectic combination of day labor, working in his father's pencil-making business, assisting Emerson in sundry ways, and land surveying. His increasingly successful surveying practice, begun in the late 1840s, eventually won back much of the local respect his unconventional choices had cost him.

Small wonder, then, that we find Thoreau answering a Harvard class agent's request for a ten-year alumni retrospective in tones both sheepish and touchy: "I don't know whether mine is a profession, or a trade, or what not." "I am a Schoolmaster, a Private Tutor, a Surveyor, a Gardener, a Farmer, a Painter—I mean a House

Painter—a Carpenter, a Mason, a Day-laborer, a Pencil-Maker, a Glass-paper Maker, a Writer, and sometimes a Poetaster. If you will act the part of Iolas," he concludes with a mock-heroic flourish, "and apply a hot iron to any of these heads, I shall be greatly obliged."[1]

Thoreau's first body of writing that survives was a batch of several dozen undergraduate essays, most of them assignments on prescribed topics like the meaning of fate, the ethics of ambition, and the question of public responsibility for education. He must have taken some pride in them, because he kept them his whole life and later affirmed that learning to write was the chief benefit of a Harvard education. At first that training proved as much impediment as impetus, however. It instilled a stiffly formal style and an overreliance on arcane erudition, as with that ponderous allusion to the labors of Hercules. Only after much trial-and-error experiment did he manage to convert his youthful owlish pedantry into a more pungent idiom.

His Harvard regimen did at least have the advantage of nurturing the partiality for aphorism that became a hallmark of his writing almost from the start. "To regret deeply is to live afresh," "Beware of all enterprises that require new clothes," "What is called eloquence in the forum is commonly found to be rhetoric in the study"— assembling such collections of memorable quotations has been a pastime for Thoreau-watchers from Emerson on down, relished alike by academics and greeting card manufacturers.[2] Aphorism is also the obvious stylistic link between Thoreau's prose and that of his great precursors in the literary essay from Seneca to Montaigne and Bacon to the contemporaries who influenced him most directly, Carlyle and Emerson. What disposed Thoreau to become one of that company in the first place, however, was the ethos or ideology of verbal expression in which classically educated Euro-American youth were then steeped, whereby writing and public speaking were seen as closely allied and directed toward moral improvement and intellectual edification.

This essentially elitist ethos also deterred him from pursuit of success in the emerging mass marketplace. He largely ignored the prudent advice on how to make his work more salable that he received from his best contact in the publishing world, New York reform journalist Horace Greeley, editor of the one antebellum newspaper with anything like national circulation. (Fortunately for him, Greeley continued to promote Thoreau's work for the rest of his life and beyond.) When lecturing to lyceum audiences it was the same. Thoreau shared Emerson's enthusiasm for the new medium; indeed, the Concord Lyceum was the one local institution he supported wholeheartedly. But he was a much more uneven performer, due to shyness aggravated by reluctance to meet audiences halfway. All too often, lecturing left him fuming that he had compromised his integrity and wasted his time casting pearls before swine. So his literary labors paid poorly, and his intellectual pursuits kept being interrupted by moneymaking exigencies. He liked to compare himself to the god Apollo forced to serve as herdsman to King Admetus—even as he also claimed, especially after *Walden*'s publication put him briefly in the limelight—to prefer the privacy and freedom of obscurity to the distractions of fame.

Thoreau's lofty view of the writer's calling should not be written off as superfluous elitist baggage, however. His best writing was a direct result of the synthesis he eventually forged between the ethic of purposefulness imbibed from his schooling and his later exposure to Romantic and Transcendentalist theories of creative expression as social prophecy. Both nurtured an intensified version of the much more elastic conception of "literary" accomplishment that prevailed in the nineteenth century compared to modern times, the mark of which was not belletristic finesse but compelling expression in whatever form, from poetry to homily to social theory to science writing. This ethos was admirably suited to an aspiring writer with a penchant for intellectual prose whose talents stretched far beyond writing per se.

By a combination of temperament and necessity, Thoreau became a kind of village Leonardo, versed in an astonishing number of kinds of performance and fabrication. He was a skilled carpenter and furniture maker who, as surveyor, became a first-rate draftsman and mapmaker. For the family business, he devised innovative processing techniques that secured the Thoreaus' prosperity. In the creative and performing arts, he was drawn not only to literature but in many other directions. He was an avid dancer and an acrobatic ice-skater, and a lover of popular and classical music. He sang with gusto and loved to play the flute, both for solitary solace and for friends, composing original pieces for it as well. The pleasure the poet Milton took in the bass viol seemed to him the mark of a kindred spirit. He was also a connoisseur of landscape aesthetics who never tired of recording the minute gradations of shade, color, density, and texture of sunsets beheld from favorite hillside perches. His *Journal* is packed with such epicurean touches as "I require that the rocks over which [a brook] falls be agreeably disposed, & prefer that they be covered with lichens."[3] Such hypersensitive responsiveness to the natural world was inseparable from, though it also sometimes clashed with, his increasingly disciplined fieldwork and reading in botany, geology, hydrology, and other branches of natural and applied science.

The conception of literary genius arising from multiform energies and abilities underlies *Walden's* distinctive montage of lyric prose, memoir, do-it-yourself manual, nature description, and philosophic treatise on the essentials of economy and the meaning of life—just as it also helped catalyze such other landmark hybrids of the era as Whitman's free-verse prophetic poetry, the antislavery apocalypticism of Harriet Beecher Stowe's *Uncle Tom's Cabin*, and the fusion of metaphysical quest-romance, social anatomy, and whaling exposition in Melville's *Moby-Dick*. But that the underlying ethos was more an authorizing vision than a specific literary recipe prolonged the time it took all these writers to reach literary maturity—for Thoreau, more than a decade.

Thoreau inherited this flute from his older brother John. He loved to play the flute both alone and in company, composing music for it as well. *Walden* playfully recalls charming the fishes of the pond like a homespun Orpheus, and Louisa May Alcott celebrates his prowess in her poem "Thoreau's Flute." *By permission of the Concord Museum.*

To tease out *Walden*'s coy allusion to the various "enterprises I have cherished," here were some of his early literary ventures. In his twenties, he put much energy into poetry, eventually composing more than two hundred poems overall, of which a goodly number appeared in the Transcendentalist quarterly *The Dial* (1840–44) and many more in *A Week* and later works. Most were workmanlike at best, doggerel at worst, but with a few gems interspersed, most of them in a ruminatively cerebral vein. Two of the best are a short apostrophe to rising smoke ("Light-winged Smoke, Icarian bird'"), which found its way into *Walden*,[4] and the seven-stanza "Sic Vita" (1841), which likens the speaker's waywardness to the bouquet it both describes and imitates in shape:

I am a parcel of vain strivings tied
     By a chance bond together,
Dangling this way and that, their links
       Were made so loose and wide,
             Methinks,
     For milder weather.[5]

During the years he was most active as a poet, Thoreau also undertook a compendious study of English poetry from the Middle Ages through the eighteenth century, possibly with the notion of an anthology in mind. At Emerson's prompting, he also translated several Greek and Latin authors for *The Dial*—his translation of Aeschylus's *Prometheus Bound* did service for a while as a trot for Harvard students—as well as a series of "Ethnical Scriptures," excerpts culled from classic Chinese, Indic, and Islamic texts whose pithy moralism reinforced his disposition for scripture-like pronouncement.

All this time, Thoreau was also experimenting with essays in different registers from the didactic to the rhapsodic to the jaunty and satiric as magazine pieces or lecture scripts. During the eight years between leaving Harvard and moving to Walden, his portfolio expanded to include disquisitions on soldierly staunchness, sound and silence, and reform culture; sketches of a winter stroll, a prototypical tavern-keeper, and the natural and cultural history of Concord River; and profiles of Walter Raleigh and Thomas Carlyle. The voluminous journal he began after meeting Emerson in 1837 became a repository of first thoughts and early drafts for many of these efforts.

Thoreau's closest literary acquaintances—Fuller, Hawthorne, Bronson Alcott, and especially Emerson—supported his early efforts but were understandably less impressed by them than by his emphatic personality. Not until Greeley took Thoreau under his wing during an unhappy summer in New York as resident tutor to Emerson's brother's sons (1843) did Thoreau begin making a little money from his pen. Even then, the conviction that art worthy of the name turned on a fusion of deep original thought and life-experience from which style and form should follow naturally hampered him from thinking in practical terms about writing as a craft. It drew him to metaphors of literary creation as part of an expanded field of artisanal interaction with the physical world that said little about the toolkit required. The labor of writing imagined as plowing a straight furrow or striking an

expert blow of the ax; a page of text "with as true & inevitable a meaning as a hill-side"; a book whose leaves "shall push out with the skunk
cabbage in the spring"—these were a few of his typical similitudes.
Small wonder that well into his thirties we find Thoreau lamenting,
"I feel myself uncommonly prepared for *some* literary work, but I can
select no work."[6]

In the end, his literary maturation hinged, unsurprisingly, on
fusion of the two templates in which he had been most deeply satu-
rated from youth: the essay, whose basics he had mastered in school,
and travel writing—narratives by explorers, discoverers, missionaries, scientists, ethnographers, adventurers. Champlain's *Voyages*,
William Bartram's *Travels* in Florida, William Ellis's *Polynesian
Researches*, Alexander von Humboldt's *Travels*, Charles Darwin's
Voyage of the Beagle—such was his favorite discretionary reading
from his undergraduate years onward and the modern literary genre
with which he tried hardest to keep up. Essay and travel narrative
also lent themselves to hybridization. Essay was a loose container
with great latitude for narrative asides; travel narrative allowed for
long stretches of rumination.

The four books Thoreau published or nearly finished in his lifetime take full advantage of this flexibility: *A Week on the Concord and
Merrimack Rivers* (planned and written 1841–49), *Walden* (1845–
54), *The Maine Woods* (1848–62), and *Cape Cod* (1849–62). All
center on the author's foragings around the New England region,
interweaving narrative, description, and essay. He infuses all with a
sense of mythic questing that hovers between epic and mock-epic
and repeatedly analogizes between the scene at hand and counter-
parts remote in space and time culled from voyages through the
realms of books and imagination. Since *Walden* has been discussed
extensively above, we'll concentrate on the other three here.

Thoreau's first book, *A Week on the Concord and Merrimack Rivers*
(1849), was the most intellectually ambitious of the four, more so even
than *Walden*, although his least successful synthesis of disparate materials. Its seven chapters ("Saturday" to "Friday") follow the riverine

parts of the Thoreau brothers' 1839 trip by water and land to the top of New England's highest peak, Mt. Washington in New Hampshire's White Mountains. Building on the work of such Romantic fellow-travelers as Goethe, Wordsworth, and Fuller, Thoreau pushes to the limit the genre's openness to philosophic digression.

Indeed, nothing in American travel literature, factual or fictional, matches *A Week*'s extravagance except Melville's novels *Moby-Dick* and *Mardi*. Its temporal range is immense, comprehending the whole course of world history and myth extending back from the two centuries of New England's settlement to the Indigenous dispensations before it, the Greco-Roman dawn of Western culture, human civilization's still remoter Indic roots, even to Adam and Eve. Geographically, the author's gaze roams far afield to encompass the whole Concord-Merrimack watershed from its tributaries to its estuary as well as inland to other remembered sorties—ancillary quests, as it were—to the western verge of New England and beyond. Along the way he pauses to hold forth on the relative merits of Judeo-Christianity, paganism, and Hinduism; on the contemplative life versus the Western work ethic; and on the course of Western poetry from Greek epic to Roman lyric and satire to English poets from Chaucer to the near present. All told, *A Week* stands as Thoreau's closest approximation to the panoramic effect of an Emerson lecture or essay series: a succession of wide-angled heterodox takes on a dozen meaty topics in light of the postulates of universal human nature and infinite human potential. Its topics often mirror Emerson's too: History, Religion, Nature, Poetry, Heroism, Friendship, Civilization.

The downside of these multiple trajectories is an overload of underassimilated sidebars. Perilously like an anthology of the shorter works of Henry Thoreau, a waggish critic once remarked. Much of the expansion evidently happened during the two-year stretch when he was anxiously shopping the project around, after completing the first draft at Walden. Uneven though it is, however, *A Week* looms large in Thoreau's literary career as the culmination of

his apprenticeship and literary Transcendentalism's most intellectually venturesome effort.

Perhaps most distinctly Thoreauvian here is the grounding,
however precariously, of multiple speculative trajectories in a narrative anchored in place and time. *A Week*'s sense of the coevolu-
tion of natural and social landscapes is a particularly helpful key to
his later books. *A Week* delivers Thoreau's most expansive account
of the reciprocities of geography and settlement across eras, from
Native and settler dependence on river transport, to the founding
of and growth of riparian settlements, to early watershed manage-
ment by dams and canals to facilitate settlement and trade, to the
supersession of the canal system by railroads serving burgeoning
factory towns in a fast-urbanizing region. Thoreau's later work tends
to presume rather than dramatize the sense of inhabiting a region of
booming industrial growth and suburban expansion, tempting readers to underestimate his awareness of such matters. The placement
of the brother-travelers within the modernizing scene the book
surveys explains why. It makes clear that Thoreau understands the
new techno-social order perfectly well but purposely opts for the
old-fashioned ways, for traveling in a homemade sailboat by water,
overland on foot. With this he begins to stake out his later position
as advocate for cultural and ecological memory, for the kinds of
landwise and artisanal prowess that the advance of modernization
threatens to eclipse.

Historical geography is more *A Week*'s context than its subject
proper, however. Its energies are largely channeled into the chronicle of the trip and the many sidebars, of which the longest, most
provocative, and most revealing biographically is a disquisition on
friendship at the book's center.

Thoreau's theory of friendship pushes to extremes the Aristotelian
notion of an ideal *philia* as virtue's foundation. In principle, friendship is based on complete frankness of mutual disclosure and nurtures
emotional and spiritual elevation on both sides. In practice, inhibition, fallibility, rivalry in aspiration, and the duty to chide friends

for failings as fiercely as to love them make the ideal unsustainable. ("Perhaps there are none charitable, none disinterested, none wise, novel, and heroic enough, for a true and lasting Friendship.")[7] Here Thoreau almost certainly had in mind the two men with whom he had been closest, concerning whom this section seems an act of invocation, farewell, and exorcism wrapped into one. One was his brother and fellow voyager, who is invoked at the outset as the book's muse, whose early death from tetanus had devastated him, whom he never ceased to mourn. John was also, however, the charismatic elder sibling from whose shadow he must now emerge by memorializing their excursion quest-romance style.

The other is Emerson, whose own essay "Friendship" in *Essays, First Series* Thoreau echoes repeatedly, but distances himself from in the process. Especially telling is the contrast between Emerson's valuation of friendship as a stimulus to one's own elevation versus the importance Thoreau attaches to mutuality. Emerson's professed readiness to show friends the door when they start annoying the busy sage with private grievances is mirrored by the restive disciple's frustration at friendship quashed by miscommunication.

That divergence anticipates what soon happened in life. *A Week*'s commercial failure, leaving Thoreau with a debt to his publisher that took years to pay off, precipitated a disenchantment with Emerson that never fully healed when Thoreau concluded that his mentor had withheld reservations about the book even while urging him to publish. So *A Week* proved a turning point for Thoreau in two senses: a culmination of his Transcendentalist apprenticeship and a jolt that sent him on a more independent course.

A Week was an aspiring author's effort to achieve maximum possible scope. *Walden* was a work of controlled mastery. During the nine years he worked on it (1845–54), Thoreau became a much more self-exacting craftsman. *Walden* achieves a far more disciplined, subtle, and pungent synthesis of narrative and essayistic elements. Essayistic reflections on defining aspects of the author's experience, often in pairs, arise more logically from the flow of the narrative ("Solitude" and "Visitors," "Bean Field" and "Village," "Higher Laws" and "Brute Neighbors"); and the chronicle of homesteading through the seasons takes root, shape, and momentum from the two opening chapters that set forth, in turn, the underlying practical and spiritual motives for the experiment.

Walden's manifold strengths and canonical status make it tempting and up to a point legitimate to think of it not only as Thoreau's most accomplished literary work but also as the centerpiece of his entire work and thought. There are also good reasons for resisting that temptation, however. One is the sheer intellectual range and audacity of its predecessor, however uneven the result. Moreover, *Walden* was by no means Thoreau's only other subsequent major literary project. Nor is it clear that he set much greater store by it than he did by the other books he designed but never completed, not to mention his *Journal*, which some Thoreauvians believe to be his very greatest literary achievement.

That Thoreau took almost a decade to finish *Walden* was partly because his attention was divided between it and several other substantial literary undertakings, not counting *A Week*, which he finished while composing *Walden*'s early drafts. These were write-ups of excursions to Maine, Cape Cod, and Francophone Canada. Taken together, they make clear the seriousness of his ongoing investment in narratives of travel farther afield. Admittedly, his initial reason for leveraging his writing time between *Walden* and travels elsewhere was probably as much pragmatic as intrinsic, namely their potential as lecture and magazine fare. "Excursion to Canada" (aka "A Yankee in Canada") is the clearest case: a potboiler he soon disowned as mediocre. But the two books published posthumously as *The Maine Woods* and *Cape Cod* became much more ambitious affairs. Their narrative flair, their keen aesthetic eye, the research that both books bring to bear in charting the two regions' natural and cultural histories, their shrewd predictions of the likely futures of both—all this has made them the most durable literary classics on their mutually disparate peripheries of New England.

Both were based on several visits spaced some years apart, in most cases with a traveling companion Thoreau knew well. *The Maine Woods* presents the three accounts seriatim (1846, 1853, 1857), the first two of them lightly revised versions of magazine pieces. *Cape Cod* synthesizes his four sorties (1849–57) into a ten-chapter sequence that follows the itinerary of the initial trip to and down the Cape first by rail, then stagecoach, then on foot.

Upcountry Maine attracted Thoreau as New England's equivalent of the American West, its immense tracts of uncut woods populated mostly by roaming lumbermen, trappers, and Native peoples. Read in sequence, the three parts of *The Maine Woods* showcase the gradual shift in Thoreau's later writing from the thoughts and movements of the perceiver to the more objectified rendering of place over time confirmed and accentuated by the two later unfinished book projects to be discussed in the next chapter.

Part I, "Ktaadn" (1848), is Thoreau's most striking effort in the romantic mountaineering vein, essentially of a piece with "A Walk to Wachusett" and the epiphanic mountaintop overnight cameo in the "Tuesday" chapter of *A Week*. Its climax, a failed ascent of New England's second highest peak, has been a touchstone for contested interpretations of Thoreau's reaction to wilderness as against wildness. The awestruck adventurer is rebuffed by a forbiddingly rocky and beclouded landscape that seems to personify a hostile nature, a disconcertingly different avatar from the tamer ones of home. Thoreauvians differ as to whether to take this portion of "Ktaadn" as a confession of inability to cope with actual wilderness or as a literary tour de force in the tradition of the romantic sublime, or a combination of the two—an awakening, one reader suggests, to the "brute facticity" of physical nature jarring at the time but crucial in propelling him away from Emersonian idealism.[8] At all events, the author's acknowledgment of disorientation upon venturing beyond his comfort zone underscores his declared preference for the settled landscapes more familiar to him.

The climax of "Ktaadn" rises up like the craggy mountain itself from a more methodical account of itinerary, environmental description, and camping pragmatics that follows the traveling party's movements stage by stage. This anticipates the comparative granularity of *Walden*'s second major phase of composition and of *The Maine Woods*' ensuing parts: "Chesuncook" and "Allegash and East Branch." These too are infused by a mix of excitement and anxiety at venturing into true wilderness that dwarfs the pocket-sized remnants Thoreau has in mind when prescribing "the tonic of wildness" as nurture for the soul in *Walden*,[9] but with a firmer grasp of Maine's ecology and history, especially two related concerns that "Ktaadn" treats only sketchily. One is the lifeways of Maine's Native peoples, chiefly exemplified by his Penobscot guides and the settlement where they live. More on that in Chapter 5. The other, the book's more fundamental unifying thread, is the perception of wilderness country in the early stages of being tamed by canals, timbering, roadways, railroads, isolated hostelries developing into villages and towns. This surfaces with special poignancy in "Chesuncook", Thoreau's most overtly environmentalist work published in his lifetime. The trip centers on a moose hunt, carried out by his traveling companions to his horrified fascination, that looms up for him as an epitome of settler culture's thoughtless wastage. Counterpoint to this is his enthusiasm for Maine's vast remaining stretches of uncut fir, spruce, and pine, culminating in a farsighted call for the creation of national forest preserves "far in the recesses of the wilderness"[10]—a call that John Muir and other founders of organized American environmentalism would reissue a generation later.

Cape Cod is a frontier book of a very different kind. Its prevailing tone, a blend of stoicism and satire, has led some readers to think of it as a later-life voice, though it was well underway before *Walden* was done. The first sight that greets Thoreau and his companion upon reaching the coast, even before reaching the Cape proper, is a recent shipwreck, with corpses and traumatized survivors scattered about—a scene made all the more striking by the observer's impassive-seeming reaction. If oceanic destructiveness is Nature's law, he muses, "why waste any time in awe or pity?"[11] Memories of shipwrecks past persist throughout the book, in tandem with the sound of the formidable, ever-pounding sea, the desolate landscapes of dwarfish trees and depleted soil, and initially wretched weather. All this imparts an air of fatalism, reinforced by historical circumstance. Most of the parts of the Cape where Thoreau lingers longest were in decline, after salt production and whaling had tailed off and before the rise of tourism. In three of its outermost four towns, which get the lion's share of his attention, population was dwindling, not to recover until the late twentieth century.

The sense of cultural and ecological decline, except for the busy port of Provincetown at the Cape's tip, plays into Thoreau's penchant for satirizing the pretensions of settler heritage then on the rise throughout New England. He respects the probity of the long-term inhabitants, who boast its purest mixture of Pilgrim stock anywhere in America, but not their provincialism. Most of them he considers bumpkinish. Another way he cuts his fellow ethnics down to size is via a heap of documentary extracts, which would surely have been winnowed had he lived to finish the book, proving that the half-millennium of North America's "ante-Pilgrim" Euro-discoverers from the Norse to the French were navigators and explorers far superior and more daring than the English.[12]

Concurrent with this satirical thrust, however, is the author's awakening to the Cape's biodiversity; to its subtler nuances of landscape; and to the grit and sagacity of the ordinary folk who snatch a precarious living from the sea. Evocations of more enticing vistas, sometimes astonishingly beautiful, begin to offset the sandy bleakness, like the rich autumnal carpet of shrubs and cranberry bogs. The ever-threatening sea itself starts to seem as invigorating as dangerous. Whereas *The Maine Woods* consolidates its depictions by multiple loops out to strange territory and back again, the narrator's perspective in *Cape Cod* unfolds gradually over the course of the book from a kind of embattled guardedness to a more secure and receptive anchorage in these novel surroundings so different from his own, although he never drops the mask of critical ethnographer.

The time Thoreau spent planning and composing *A Week*, *Walden*, *The Maine Woods*, and *Cape Cod* spanned nearly his whole literary career, from his first sketchy jottings after his Concord-Merrimack junket to deathbed tinkering on the two he never quite finished. Underpinning them all and everything else he published, however, was the journal he kept for his whole working life. The importance he attached to it is confirmed by the thousands of passages, short and long, that he wove into lectures and his published work; by the many affirmations sprinkled throughout it of the superior authenticity and freshness of journal impressions to published distillations; and, most of all, by the sheer perseverance that maintaining it required.

Far more than Thoreau's partiality for excursion narrative, his attraction to the journal genre marks him as a child of Transcendentalism. Most leading Transcendentalists were voluminous journalizers—Emerson, Alcott, Fuller, Parker—all of them in this respect heirs of the Protestant tradition of self-examination the first Anglo-settlers of New England brought with them to the New World. That Thoreau evidently began his at Emerson's instigation, then sustained it under his own steam, was a symbolic acceptance of the mantle.

At first Thoreau treated his journal rather as Emerson did, as a miscellaneous repository for thoughts and experiences, self-assessments, reading notes, and observations on history and current events. Then it seems to have become chiefly a workbook for drafts, large chunks of which were discarded. From late 1850 onward, however, not long after *A Week* failed and concurrent with his turn toward serious study of natural history, the *Journal* took on a life of its own. "The major document of his imaginative life," its editors rightly call it, with daily dated chronicles of field observations as the backbone, often revisited and revised, though still liberally interspersed with the aforementioned ingredients.[13]

This 1856 portrait is likely the most faithful image of the later Thoreau, although it was taken at a time when he had been suffering through a prolonged bout of ill health. Daguerreotype by Benjamin D. Maxham. *National Portrait Gallery.*

Few readers, even Thoreau scholars, have mustered the patience and stamina to peruse closely this third and by far longest portion of Thoreau's *Journal* from start to finish—seven-eighths of the whole surviving text. Given the typical entry's minute particularity of item-ization, most will prefer to access the later *Journal* though abridg-ments and excerpts. An excerpting approach has the obvious upside of highlighting hundreds of tours de force that otherwise might escape notice—an experience of semimystical rapport with a wood-chuck; the excited discovery of a beautiful flower in a swamp recess to which a reluctant local led him after much cajoling; indignation at the felling of a historic elm tree that seemed a worthier citizen of Concord than the choppers and bystanders; a semidefiant confes-sion of having once accidentally set fire to the woods; unexpected glimpses of personal and family history; outbursts of uninhibited rage at the mendacity of politicians and the opportunism of greedy landowners; periodic wistful and poignant stock-takings as he feels himself aging.

An excerpting approach, however, yields a gallery of set-pieces that cannot hope to capture the complex feel of a sinuous, sinewy, omni-curious mind always in motion. In this the *Journal* comes closer than any of Thoreau's published work to rendering what was arguably his core literary aspiration all along: the "sustained process of perceiving and thinking," as one Thoreau scholar sums up; or, as another puts it with an extravagance that befits the scale of the attempt: "the thrilling disorganization of natural life that he wants poetry to be adequate to."[14] That sense of restlessly inquisitive unas-similable energies has given rise to such divergent claims for this most massive of all Thoreau's writings as a spiritual journal in the long post-Reformation turn from theocentrism to natural piety; as a showcase of scientific induction from empirical evidence ahead of its time; and as an attempted rendering of the natural world in words, superior to *Walden* and his other published books for its awareness of the limits of the graspable.[15] Such macroperspectives inevitably oversimplify the *Journal* in grasping it by a single handle. But they also model the kind of longitudinal immersion necessary to begin to fathom so vast a work. For that, ideally at least a year's worth of attentive perusal is necessary, at the bare minimum a season's.

Even a short sequence chosen at random (in this case from the winter of 1857–58) can give a flavor of the complex motions of the journalizing mind, however. One multilayered late-December entry opens with a rundown of a winter walk that includes precise mapping of mouse tracks on snow and, later on, measurements of a deceptively thin stem of a blueberry bush (diameter = $1\frac{5}{16}$ inches) whose rings prove it a remarkable twenty-nine years old. Interrupting that, however, is a lengthy rumination triggered by the distant barking of dogs at night (which produces "the same effect on fresh and healthy ears that the rarest music does," even to the point of deflecting a person from thoughts of suicide!). And sandwiched within *that* is a still more freakish detour back to a boyhood memory of his mother fashioning the pockets of his clothing from his father's old "fire-bags," which somehow reminds him of nineteenth-century recycling of tales from Greek mythology.[16]

The next two entries, by contrast, take shape as a two-part sequence of mini-essays arising from an intensive stretch of recent surveying. The first features terse profiles of various employers in descending order from the worthy to the unworthy, with his ex-jailer Sam Staples topping the list. The following entry rises from a burst of frustrated indignation at how staking out the woods cramps the mind to a sense of wonder at "What a history this Concord wilderness which I affect so much may have had!" and its making and remaking over the centuries as the land changed hands. After that the *Journal* reverts for a while to some days of relatively routine rambles. But only for a while. Those who stick with it and resist the temptation to skim—rationing oneself to a week's worth at one sitting is a useful discipline—will find in this "meteorological journal of the mind," as Thoreau once termed it, the best of all possible keys to the Concord Leonardo's thoughts, passions, art, and life.[17]

Chapter 5

The Turn to Science

Thoreau's first biographer, Ellery Channing, dubbed his friend and walking companion a "poet-naturalist."[1] The epithet has a quaintly Victorian ring, but well into the 1900s it remained a favored rubric, perhaps both despite and because it finessed the underlying question: To what extent did the poet in him give way in time to the man of science? To what extent did his attraction to the natural world shift from a romantic enthusiasm for nature as a source of spiritual renewal and literary inspiration to a disciplined commitment to empirical study of botany, phenology, and other branches of natural science?

That some such shift took place during the last dozen years of Thoreau's life has always been known. For a century after his death, however, it was little discussed beyond mining the late *Journal* for selected passages of natural history observation. Literature scholars, then and now the largest contingent of academic Thoreauvians, generally treated Thoreau's post-*Walden* years as a falling off in creative energy and output. Starting in the mid-1900s but especially since the publication of his two major late unfinished manuscripts, "The Dispersion of Seeds" (1993) and "Wild Fruits" (1999), scholars have paid much more concentrated and respectful attention to Thoreau's contributions to the history of science and technology, strengthening earlier claims for him as a natural scientist and pioneer ecologist and advancing new ones for the importance of his accomplishments in the physical and applied sciences.

Thoreau stands out among the Transcendentalists in always having taken for granted the necessity of understanding tools, machines, and quantification. Emerson, an ex-cleric descended from a tribe of ministers, felt no obligation to learn how machines worked, or even to learn the use of tools. As his father's son and apprentice, Thoreau had to; and as an inveterate tinkerer he wanted to. He built his own boats, took pride in fashioning his cabin from recycled materials, and in *Walden* consistently praises learning by doing, be it navigation or lens-grinding. He enjoyed touring the new mills and manufactories around the region, insisting after one such visit that "it should be a part of every man's education today to understand the Steam Engine."[2] His decision about this same time to become a land surveyor, probably in order to pay off the debt owed to his publisher because of *A Week*'s anemic sales, made perfect sense for one of such talents who loved the outdoors.

Thoreau's interest in the sciences as an arena of study and research developed more slowly from an early passion for what the Victorians came to call the romance of natural history—assembling collections of striking natural objects and artifacts—that Henry shared with his brother John and that also became one of the bonds of affinity between him and Ellen Sewall, the woman both brothers briefly courted.[3] In the same vein was Thoreau's first publication in this area, a review essay on "The Natural History of Massachusetts" (1842) that consisted mainly of artful cameos culled from his journal of creatures he had observed in the field. In keeping with that literary emphasis, it celebrates the "elixir" effect of old-fashioned natural history writing and condescends to the batch of reports he had been assigned to review on the state's fish, reptiles, insects, and animals as dealing "much in measurements and minute descriptions, not interesting to the general reader."[4] Later on, as his own commitment to understanding nature's workings deepened, he came to rely on such compilations, including some of the same books he had sniffed at, although he never ceased to praise the superiority of the "lively and lifelike descriptions" of "old naturalists" at the expense of

the blinkered literalism of manuals whose authors "have not imagined the actual beasts which they presume to describe."[5]

Nonetheless, Thoreau became increasingly drawn toward objective observation and experiment. Throughout his later *Journal* are
reports of thousands of field experiments from the trivial-folksy
(comparing the taste of white, black, and paper birch sap), to the
laboriously intricate: temperature readings in midsummer 1860 of
Concord rivers, brooks, springs, ponds, and swamps correlated on
the one hand with air temperature (daily and mean annual) and, on
the other, with the behavior of farmers, fish, and sundry other human
and animal populations. Not long after he left Walden, he started to
read widely in botany, geology, and other branches of natural science. He also became networked into Boston's scientific community, first as a specimen collector of turtles, fish, invertebrates, and
insects for Louis Agassiz and others. Then, on the strength of that
and his donation of a goshawk shot by a local farmer, the Boston
Society of Natural History elected him a corresponding member.
Thereafter Thoreau made frequent use of its collections and library,
also contributing specimens and at least one report of a rare sight-
ing, a Canada lynx shot in a neighboring town. After his death, the
society endorsed a tribute to him as an "eminent naturalist" by geologist Charles T. Jackson, Lidian Emerson's brother.[6] This was more
than mere politesse. His appointment to Harvard's Committee for
Examination in Natural History a few years earlier had marked his
acceptance as "officially part of the scientific establishment."[7]

What led Thoreau to devote a large percentage of his energies
from the late 1840s onward to acquiring a working knowledge of
natural science and to an increasingly intensive regime of field study?
One key motivation, perhaps the most important, was the desire to
attain a comprehensive, integrated grasp of his home region's natural phenomena through the seasons: plants, animals, invertebrates,
vicissitudes of temperature and precipitation. The second and final
major round of revisions to *Walden* reflects the liftoff phase, which
started with the records Thoreau began keeping during the sojourn

itself of snowfall, ice, and when the pond and river froze over in winter and reopened in spring. A culminating embodiment was the "Kalendar," as he sometimes called it, that he began constructing toward the end of his life to chart salient botanical and meteorological phenomena month by month from 1852 to 1861.

Thoreau's phenological observations over more than a dozen years—synthesizing his own laborious measurements, testimony from landwise neighbors, and others' research—whetted his interest in longer-term shifts in the rhythm of the seasons, including a glimmering if imperfect awareness of the phenomenon of climate warming over time. He came to realize, for example, that local temperatures had risen since the time of Concord's settlement, although he lacked the means of specifying how much or distinguishing cyclical from anthropogenic causes. Today his *Journal*, from whose observations the "Kalendar" was synthesized, serves as a valued resource for life-scientists studying the history of the plants and forests of the Northeast and the effects of climate change.

Phenology makes a good starting point for grasping the broader scope and import of Thoreau's scientific interests for at least two reasons. First, because seasonality became an organizing principle for his study of plants, animals, birds, amphibians, invertebrates, and waterways. Beyond that, however, one quickly realizes the inseparability of Thoreau's pursuit of phenology from his fascination with seasonality as a phenomenon of human experience. That in turn makes a useful brake against the temptation to type him decisively as a scientist in the modern sense. His innumerable stabs to pinning down the seasons' "infinite degrees in their revolutions" continually intermix subjective and objective: "the decided leafiness in June," "the ridge of the summer" in mid-July; "the peculiar & interesting *Brown Season* of the spring" between melt and full thaw.[8]

Just as Thoreau continued to value writing more as a medium of moral and philosophic reflection than for literary accomplishment alone even as he became a more disciplined literary craftsman, so too with his views of science and technology. Even as his surveys won fame for their precision, he chafed against the instrumental reduction of the living landscape to geometric plots for the sake of gain. As his botanical observations became more systematic, he pushed back all the more vigorously against the defining shift then underway that marks the emergence of modern scientific practice, toward suppressing the subjective factor in the investigation of natural phenomena so as to achieve maximum objectification. He never sought to study botany as such, he declared, but simply wished to become better acquainted with his nonhuman neighbors. Here Thoreau anticipates the vision of a greater bioregional community of plants, land, and people articulated in the next century both from the side of science and from the side of creative writing by conservation ecologist Aldo Leopold, ethnobotanist Gary Paul Nabham, and poet-essayists Wendell Berry and Gary Snyder, among many others. Science mattered more as a means to understand and achieve that goal, for him and for them, than as an end in itself. Hence the complaints strewn throughout Thoreau's later *Journal* that "the character of my knowledge is from year to year becoming more distinct & scientific—that in exchange for views as wide as heaven's cope I am being narrowed down to the field of the microscope."[9] Paradoxically but predictably, such assertions intensify as his turn to science becomes more pronounced.

Thoreau's concerns about the affective cost of analytic objectivism even as he strove for greater empirical rigor make a rich case study of the experience of living at the threshold of the professionalization of science into a set of disciplines and approved methods of inquiry. Beyond that, they attest to the tribulations that can overtake earnest souls of any era or life-stage contemplating the tradeoffs that seem the necessary price of specialization. This side of Thoreau can appeal alike to idealistic youth fearful that the curiosity and wonder that drew them to their subject will be asphyxiated by obeisance to methodological rigor, and to seasoned specialists striving through narrative and memoir to transmit the excitement of discovery suppressed by the protocols of academic research articles. Equally important, however, is that Thoreau's reservations did not keep him from the pursuit of his scientific projects any more than they have for latter-day researchers with intellectual interests that range beyond their fields of specialization.

Since Thoreau came to science slowly and haltingly, it is not surprising that it took years for him to decide just where to focus his energies. An often cited but easily misunderstood 1853 *Journal* passage shows the transitional process at work: Thoreau's tart reaction to a question on a survey from the American Association for the Advancement of Science as to "what branch of science I was specially interested in." A sincere answer, he declares, would have made him "the laughing stock of the scientific community," since "they do not believe in a science which deals with the higher law." So he confined himself to "that poor part of me which alone they can understand. The fact is," he adds, "I am a mystic—a transcendentalist—& a natural philosopher to boot. Now I think of it I should have told them at once that I was a transcendentalist—that would have been the shortest way of telling them that they would not understand my explanations."[10]

Thoreauvians have often seized on this passage as evidence that he continued to regard scientific work as a lesser pursuit even as he pursued it. Its target, though, is not so much science itself as the bureaucratic proceduralism that irked him not only here but across the board, in government, in religion, even in literature. This, after all, was the same person whose life would be cut short by an excess of zeal counting tree rings in freezing December weather as part of a long-term study of local forest history. The fact is that Thoreau did dutifully complete and return his AAAS questionnaire, prompting an appointment to membership—which he declined on the ground he lived too far away to attend meetings—that confirmed his fitness for the club.

Other aspects of Thoreau's response to the survey are equally revealing. First are the models he cites, classic rather than contemporary works with a strongly literary flavor: Gilbert White's *Natural*

History of Selbourne and Alexander von Humboldt's *Views of Nature*, an eighteenth-century amateur naturalist's epistolary account of local discoveries, and a collection of resonant essays by the early nineteenth century's most celebrated polymath naturalist on natural phenomena of the tropics (waterfalls, forests, volcanoes) and their human inhabitants. Neither then nor later did Thoreau show any more relish for writing conventional scientific reports than he had for reading them.

Another sign of the transitional state of Thoreau's thinking was that he listed as his "especial interest" "The Manners & Customs of the Indians of the Algonquin Group previous to contact with the Civilized Man."[11] To characterize himself as an ethnographer made better sense in 1853 than it would have later on. Not for some years would he start concentrated work on "Dispersion," "Wild Fruits," and the "Kalendar"; but by 1853 he had filled eight of an eventual twelve manuscript notebooks with notes and excerpts from writings by Euro-American explorers, missionaries, travelers, and anthropologists about the geography, history, language, and customs of the Native peoples of the Northeast and their interaction with settler society.

This in fact was the closest approximation to a systematic freestanding megascale research project Thoreau ever undertook. It had also been the subject of his first amateurish fieldwork. Long before he took up specimen collecting for Agassiz, he was an eager collector of arrowheads and other aboriginal artifacts. Concord's location, on "*arrowheadiferous*" sandy soil where two rivers met, had been as attractive to pre-Columbian Native peoples as it was to the British settlers who seized on the place for New England's first inland town. For Thoreau, "the gold which our sands yield" seemed far more alluring than California's. He himself became an eagle-eyed prospector who prided himself on his collections. Late in life, he happily recalled "whole afternoons, esp. in the spring,—pacing back & forth over a sandy field—looking for these relics of a race."[12]

Collecting itself, however, mattered far less to him than the sense of connection with earlier human inhabitants. His relics seemed "fossil thoughts—forever reminding me of the mind that shaped them."[13] This fascination was typical of his lifelong aspiration to re-experience the foundational terms of human thought, life, civilization—as with *Walden's* doctrine of the four essential needs of subsistence, and its idealization of Homer and the wisdom of ancient Asian cultures. In similar spirit, Thoreau sifted the archives of his own ethnic forbears, the early Euro-explorers and settlers: the Jesuit *Relations*, the narratives of Champlain and John Smith, the seventeenth-century Puritan chroniclers.

Although he continued to assemble his "Indian Books" until his health failed, Thoreau showed no clear sign of wanting to work them up for publication, and they remain in manuscript to this day. Perhaps he recognized the improbability of so lococentric a person undertaking the requisite fieldwork, or of disengagement from the Eurocentric biases that he chided in his precursors but that also clouded his own vision. Even after witnessing Native Americans living in villages cannily adapting to settler ways, he could not resist imagining them as people of the woods contorted if not doomed by contact with so-called civilization.

Thoreau did progress considerably beyond the adolescent self who enjoyed playing Indian with his brother, however, as his write-ups of the three trips collected in *The Maine Woods* especially show. The first was published on the eve of his scientific turn; the second after it was well underway; the third posthumously. Read in sequence, they show the advance both of his understanding of Native culture and of the empirical turn of his later thought generally.

In Part I, Native America figures in ways peripheral and stereotypical: in the literal form of shirkers who do not show up after being hired, and the metaphorical guise of the god Pomola who guards Katahdin's summit. Parts II and III, "Chesuncook" and "Allegash and the East Branch," attend more closely to the Indigenous people and their lifeways, especially to his Native guides, in "Chesuncook" a chief's son and in "Allegash" a tribal leader in his prime.

An epiphanic moment in "Chesuncook" is the author's excited witness to a campfire exchange among a group of Indians in their own language: his awakening to the sense of Native culture as a living culture.[14] Admiration for the topographical and toponymic nuance of Algonquian languages underlies the "List of Indian Words" at the book's end that combines gleanings from Native guides with Thoreau's reading. Sizable parts of "Allegash" in particular are devoted to informal ethnography, including one of the era's fullest portraits of an individual Native American by a nineteenth-century Euro-American writer, Thoreau's guide Joseph Polis, whom he obviously respected far more than his previous guide.

Perhaps the most telling mark of Thoreau's respect, however, was his refusal to publish "Allegash" in his lifetime on the chance the literate Polis might read it. For "Allegash" is also suffused with settler-culture prejudice, chiding Polis for being superstitious, wasteful, complaining when sick ("like the Irish").[15] Significantly, his cross-cultural adroitness interests Thoreau far less than his woodsmanship—his uncanny ability to spot seemingly invisible paths, make tea from an unending array of trees and plants, and make himself at home in the forest even when he does not know exactly where he is. This tempts Thoreau in turn to display his own expertise in a series of entertaining head-to-head scenes where the guide figures by turns as tutor and bemused rival in canoeing, foot-racing along paths while carrying gear, and so forth. Thoreau relates these episodes, however, not as a memoir of personal relations across the red-white divide but as an encounter with a remarkable specimen of Native culture, almost always referring to Polis as "The Indian," although he and his companion called him by name on the trip itself.

It was well, then, that Thoreau's fascination with aboriginal culture and the Maine woods remained more a side interest than a primary pursuit. He was far better equipped for investigation of the natural and cultural history of his home region. By the time he returned the AAAS survey he was on his way to a more comprehensive grasp of the history and ecology of Concord's woods, fields, and riverways than anyone before him—and almost anyone since.

With the unprecedented attention devoted since the 1990s to the long-neglected trove of late Thoreau manuscripts, for the first time we have begun to understand the full scale of what Emerson's funeral address grandly, rightly, but vaguely described as studies "so large as to require longevity."[16] His accomplishments in scientific investigation, as a quantitative thinker and doer, have been shown to be more extensive and as mattering more deeply to him than had ever been supposed; and that in turn has prompted new claims about the relative importance of his "poetic" and "naturalist" sides.

A striking case in point is geologist Robert Thorson's reappraisal in *Walden's Shore* of Thoreau's *Journal* during the several-year runup to *Walden* after it abruptly shifted, in November 1850, from a compendium of events, thoughts, and impressions into the much more systematic detailed write-ups of his regime of daily walks and field observations that it largely remained for the rest of his life. Here, Thorson declares, we see the impetus behind the Walden "upgrade," that is, the fleshing-out of concentrated empirical observation of the Walden environment by contrast to the much sparser earlier drafts. Whereas Thoreauvians of literary bent often find his later *Journal* a tedious tangle to be skimmed for intermittent luminous aperçus, Thorson perceives the disciplined energy and excitement behind the welter of measurements and catalogings. This as he sees it was Thoreau's crucial emergence point as a scientific investigator in the modern sense. Thereafter, "Thoreau walked like a field scientist, carried the equipment of a field scientist, read scientific articles and texts on field science, and made important new discoveries based on field evidence."[17]

Here and in a successor study, *The Boatman: Henry Thoreau's River Years*, Thorson contends no less vehemently, and on the whole persuasively, that Thoreau's range of scientific and technical interests and accomplishments was far more extensive than anyone previously thought. Thoreau was a pioneering geoscientist whose lifelong interest in rivers also propelled him to the forefront of contemporary hydrology and river geomorphology. *The Boatman's* account of Thoreau's involvement in the long debate over the impact of raising the Billerica Dam in the early 1800s on the Concord River makes it also the most searching investigation to date of Thoreau's position as diagnostician of the "highly disrupted Anthropocene landscape" that his region had increasingly become in his lifetime.[18]

The attention this and other studies have called to Thoreau's meticulous map of the Concord River system, made near the end of his life after being drawn briefly into a lawsuit by a group of aggrieved farmers who sued to have the dam level lowered, exemplifies how twenty-first-century Thoreauvians of all stripes have been sifting his late manuscripts in order to reassess his scientific and technical achievements. Revaluation of Thoreau's career as professional surveyor is another example. Until recently, most Thoreauvians took pretty much at face value his complaints about surveying as

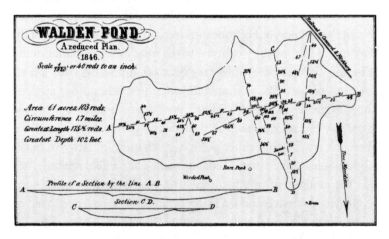

This somewhat simplified version of Thoreau's survey of Walden Pond was printed in the first edition of Walden (*Wa* 286) near the start of "The Pond in Winter," which summarizes his measurements and reflects on their symbolic significance.

LAND SURVEYING

Of all kinds, according to the best

methods known; the necessary data supplied, in order that the boundaries of Farms may be accurately described in Deeds; *Woods* lotted off distinctly and according to a regular plan; *Roads* laid out, &c., &c. Distinct and accurate Plans of Farms furnished, with the buildings thereon, of any size, and with a scale of feet attached, to accompany the Farm Book, so that the land may be laid out in a winter evening.

Areas warranted accurate within almost any degree of exactness, and the Variation of the Compass given, so that the lines can be run again. Apply to

HENRY D. THOREAU,

near the Depot
Concord Mass

This handbill for posting and circulation was likely written by Thoreau himself. It shows his customary passion for precision and supports his claim that "I have always endeavored to acquire strict business habits" (*Wa* 20). Critic of capitalism though he was, Thoreau was an efficient businessman when he set his mind to it. *New York Public Library: Berg Collection of English and American Literature.*

necessary but irritating day labor. His survey of the pond's depth and breadth, inserted into the first edition of *Walden*, was written off as a puzzling eccentricity, perhaps even a jest, rather than as the certified professional's demonstration of the mathematical basis of his philosophical claims about the correspondence between the natural and ethical domains that it was almost surely intended to be. Today the pride Thoreau took in the honesty and precision of his work and the respect it won him are better appreciated, and his portfolio of survey commissions now looms up as a substantial accomplishment in its own right.

Among the branches of science in which Thoreau became versed, however, the one that drew him most strongly and commanded the largest share of his reading and fieldwork was the first area in which his scientific contributions were recognized: plant biology. It makes sense that he called himself a "botanist" when he wanted something more precise than the omnibus term naturalist. His two most extensive late manuscripts, "The Dispersion of Seeds" and "Wild Fruits," both certainly books in the making, were plant-centric works, as were his three most polished and successful late-life natural history lecture-essays. "Succession of Forest Trees," the one published in his lifetime, is a preliminary statement of the core finding in "Dispersion"; "Wild Apples" was a portion of the "Wild Fruits" project; and "Autumnal Tints" was a short-form crystallization of another incipient book project he had been mulling for years.

"Dispersion" and "Wild Fruits" draw from the same database as the "Kalendar": Thoreau's accrued observations, most recorded in the *Journal*, of the appearance, blossoming, fruitage, and dissemination of scores of Concord's plants from about 1850 onward. The two manuscripts point toward very different kinds of outcomes, however.

The main body of "Wild Fruits," the more inchoate, consists almost entirely of profiles of selected individual plants, shrubs, and trees arranged in sequence according to their time of fruiting. Most entries are mere placeholders, but a few are extended essays—"Black

Huckleberry" and "Wild Apple" being the most elaborate—which both describe the objective appearance of the fruit in question and expound at length on its aesthetic, medicinal, cultural-historical, and commercial values, with a generous injection of personal experience and opinion thrown in. The work as a whole seems intended as a compendium for general audiences, fellow Concordians in the first instance: a compendium with a moral, several ones in fact. It seeks to inform an increasingly urbanizing and insouciant audience not only about the botanical properties of wild fruits but also their place in human history, their aesthetic qualities, and the superiority of foraging for nature's bounty in season to market purchase. Beyond that, the author issues a call for the preservation of large tracts of nature unimpaired in every town as common space for recreation and instruction.

"The Dispersion of Seeds" is a far more scientifically ambitious project. It offers a much fuller and more complex analysis of the phenomenon of seed diffusion by wind, birds, and animals than the brief account in "The Succession of Forest Trees" of why oaks spring up in stands where conifers have been cut down and vice versa. It marshals additional evidence to support the refutation in "Successions" of such popular misconceptions as the obsolete but still-tenacious theory of spontaneous generation. It makes clear that what most fascinated Thoreau about this subject were the many random-seeming ways, imperceptible to the unpracticed eye, that the seeds of things are unobtrusively distributed by natural agents, often in unexpected places.

"Dispersion" thereby reinforces mid-twentieth-century claims based on that lecture-essay for Thoreau as a harbinger of modern forest succession. More than anything else he wrote, including the "Indian Books," it witnesses, furthermore, to the seriousness and momentum of his commitment to rigorous, sustained investigation of a specific scientific issue: to years of patient, vigilant field observation and to his assiduousness in keeping up with the available literature as long as his health allowed. Whatever else Thoreau might have gone on to achieve, he clearly made himself into a forest scientist second to none in his ability to read, as he whimsically puts it, "the rotten papyrus on which the history of the Concord forest is written."[19]

Not that "Dispersion" is pitched to a scientific community alone. "Succession" had been delivered at the Concord's annual county fair, or "cattle show," as such gatherings were then called, then published in both the *Transactions of the Middlesex Agricultural Society* and the *New York Tribune*. Like "Succession" and "Wild Fruits," "Dispersion" seeks not only to contribute to the scientific understanding of seed dispersal but also to dramatize to readers at large the fascination and subtleties of the process, as well as to reprove ignorant meddling with nature's ways, wayward though they seem. In several witty satirical thrusts, he praises the squirrels of Concord as far better stewards of its woodlots than its blundering farmers ever were.

Insofar as both "Dispersion" and "Wild Fruits" reflect the aesthetic, ethical, and spiritual promptings that drew Thoreau to nature in the first place, they seem as much outgrowths as breaks from his earlier thought and writing. Clash though they did, poet and naturalist were also mutually reinforcing avatars. The delicacy and beauty of seed structure and aerial transmission fascinated Thoreau as well as the mechanics of dispersal and were integral to many of his observations of them and how he wrote about them. His desire to fathom the workings of plant distribution and forest history was inseparable from the ethical and aesthetic sides of his proto-environmentalism. His late natural history writings are shot through with metaphor, fable, and wry humor even as the prose becomes more reportorial and the adventures of the persona subsidiary to the analysis of natural phenomena.

Conversely, Thoreau came to believe that to render subtleties of color and form in landscape painting required a trained botanical eye. As his own scientific knowledge deepened, his cameos of personal encounters with animals, trees, rivers, sunsets, skyscapes that began with "Natural History of Massachusetts" gained in beauty and subtlety as they gained in precision.

In seeking to transmit his findings in literary prose that would reach general readers as well as scientific audiences, Thoreau did not differ markedly from such groundbreaking figures of his day as Charles Lyell, Louis Agassiz, and Charles Darwin. What especially marks him as a transitional figure rather than a modernizer is his outsidership to the emerging paradigm for doing science in modern times: research conducted increasingly in collaboration with acknowledged peers whose analytical procedures and conclusions presumed a decidedly materialist understanding of scientific truth. Thoreau was too much the loner and not enough of a reductionist to fit that mold comfortably, although he was perfectly aware of the direction in which scientific work was moving and, up to a point, pursued it in his own way with considerable zeal.

A common criterion for defining Thoreau's position in the march of science is where he stood on the theory of biological evolution. Clearly he detached himself pretty quickly from the residues of Providentialism in Coleridge and Lyell in favor of the more purely naturalistic theories of Humboldt and Robert Chambers's best-selling *Vestiges of Creation* (1844). Both helped condition him to conceive the biological universe as evolving through processes wholly natural and to welcome Darwin's *Origin of Species* as a confirmation of his views, not a threat. What Thoreau thought about the most controversial part of Darwinian theory, the mutability of species itself by adaptation, is by no means clear, however. Indeed, he seems to have taken no special notice either of this landmark aspect of the theory or the firestorm it unleashed. Perhaps familiarity with earlier thinking about the metamorphosis of life forms from Goethe to Chambers led him to absorb what seemed a revolutionary claim to the scientific community at large as a minor adjustment to be taken in stride. Or, like many researchers on fire with their own current project, perhaps Thoreau read *Origin of Species* especially with an eye to its insights about species distribution, not species mutability. That would have been in keeping with how he typically sifted through his source material: "more for confirmation than discovery," as biographer Robert Richardson Jr. sums up.[20] In any case, the history of evolutionary theory is not the best standpoint from which to appreciate the accomplishments of Thoreau the naturalist.

Much more important are two other considerations. First is the sheer range of areas in which this man of letters, operating chiefly on his own, became a harbinger of modern theory and practice: geology, hydrology, civil engineering, limnology, phenology, forest science, ecology. Second is that in the latter four, even if not (yet) the others, he is widely regarded as a pioneer figure. Although Thoreau will almost certainly never loom so large in the history of natural and applied science as he does in the history of literature and political theory, what he did achieve was impressive for its day and in combination with his other accomplishments truly remarkable.

Chapter 6

The Political Thoreau

To what extent can we reconcile the Thoreau who preferred the companionship of nature to human society with the political thinker and antislavery activist who suffered imprisonment for conscience's sake? Since Thoreau's death, the sense of incompatibility has increased. Thoreau the cabin-dweller, guardian of nature, and student of natural history and the political Thoreau have often appealed to different constituencies. From our comparative analysis of *Walden* and "Civil Disobedience" it seems clear that the relationship between the political Thoreau and Thoreau the poet-naturalist was as much a symbiotic tension as a complete antithesis. Just how consistent and abiding was Thoreau's engagement in political thought and action over the course of his life, however, is much less clear.

Thoreau's enduring reputation as a political thinker and actor rests especially on a handful of lecture-essays precipitated by specific crises in the history of the American antislavery movement from the Mexican War to John Brown's raid on Harpers Ferry. This is a small fraction of the Thoreau canon but by far the most impassioned. Bridging the political writings proper and Thoreau's book-length works is another series of polemic pieces from early to late in his career that assail status quo complacency and misdirected social reform efforts and testify to a chronic distrust of any and all social institutions.

As a Harvard undergraduate, Thoreau followed institutional codes of behavior more dutifully than many of his classmates although, in his college themes, he did not hesitate to question the justice of the law and assert that "the fear of displeasing the world ought not, in the least, to influence my actions." Broadly speaking, the same held true his whole life. As his mentor Emerson summed it up at Thoreau's funeral: "he was more unlike his neighbors in his thought than in his action."[1]

Thoreau began to gain a reputation for risk-taking cantankerousness, however, long before he held forth about politics or engaged in political protest. His angry resignation within a few weeks of his appointment as town schoolmaster, soon after graduating from Harvard, gave early notice. When an old-fashioned overseer requested that he use corporal punishment for discipline, Thoreau responded with a travesty of compliance by chastising some random victims, after which he summarily abandoned his attractive first post, despite the risks of doing so in the midst of the economic Panic of 1837. The incident highlights a combination of headstrong high-mindedness and a penchant for acerbic satire that seems not to have bothered Thoreau's family in the least but sometimes made his friends wince and chide. Emerson famously remarks in his address at Thoreau's funeral on his "somewhat military" nature, as if his "first instinct on hearing as proposition was to controvert it"—a habit, Emerson slyly adds, "a little chilling to the social affections."[2]

Indeed the very first essay Thoreau worked up for publication (unsuccessfully) was a celebration of preparedness for moral struggle, "The Service"—forgettably turgid in itself, but notable as augury of a lifelong penchant for clothing the idea of moral combat in military garb. Its vague but dogged moral idealism reads like a secular version of the old Protestant hymn "Onward Christian Soldiers." From youth onward, Thoreau showed a special admiration for models of staunchness under duress: Prometheus on his rock, Carlyle the embattled and trenchant social critic, the fortitude of Walter Raleigh through his imprisonment and execution, and the courage of such antislavery radicals as Wendell Phillips who seemed motivated solely by principle, not prudence, willing to risk all for the cause. One of Thoreau's favorite poems was Raleigh's "The Soul's Errand"

("Give the world the lie!"), which he later quoted in its entirety as a tribute to John Brown.

Compared to Phillips and Brown, Thoreau's best-known deeds of defiance were intermittent and largely symbolic, including the most famous: his removal to Walden on July 4, 1845, and his night in jail the following summer. Not that he hesitated to put himself in real jeopardy at other times, as during the school discipline controversy. On the half-dozen or so known occasions when he helped fugitive slaves escape to Canada or radical white abolitionists escape pursuit by the authorities. He did so unhesitatingly, even matter-of-factly, without fret or compunction. No doubt this was due in no small part to the support of his close-knit family, all of them antislavery in a bitterly divided town. Several of the Thoreau women were founding members of Concord's first antislavery organization, and his older sister Helen became a valued associate of William Lloyd Garrison and Frederick Douglass years before Thoreau himself entered the fray.

When Thoreau did finally speak out in public against slavery, however, the results were powerful in thought if not deed. As biographer Laura Dassow Walls declares, "John Brown's sword was impressive, but without the word, it was just a sword."[3] And of all the words of political thought and advocacy inspired by the conflict over slavery, none except Lincoln's have had a more lasting impact than Thoreau's "Civil Disobedience."

The act that precipitated the essay, Thoreau's arrest for refusal to pay his poll tax, took its cue from a similar act by Bronson Alcott a few years before. Both reflected the gospel of "nonresistance" or nonviolent protest against unjust institutions advocated by the antislavery movement launched by William Lloyd Garrison, of which Alcott was a charter member. In this respect, Garrisonianism was influenced by the so-called New England Non-Resistance movement, originally formed to protest the region's involvement in the War of 1812. Its influence persisted into the 1840s, as in Emerson's 1837 lecture "War," published in the same collection as "Civil

Disobedience,"[4] and the early writing of Charles Sumner, later antislavery's foremost champion in the US Senate. The year before Thoreau's incarceration, Sumner made far more of a stir than "Civil Disobedience" would with a rousing July 4 oration in Boston that similarly disdained the customary pious drivel about the nation's revolutionary heritage, asserting that "in our age . . . there can be no war that is not dishonorable."[5]

In "Civil Disobedience," however, Thoreau frames his own protest not simply as a nonviolent disavowal of a corrupt regime waging an unjust war in order to expand the unjust institution of slavery, but also, more pugnaciously, as an act of resistance justified by the right of revolution in the spirit of 1776. Thoreau's changes in title over time mirror the instability of this synthesis: first the neutral-sounding "Rights and Duties of the Individual in Relation to the State" and "The Relation of the Individual to the State" for his public lectures; then "Resistance to Civil Government," the confrontational title of the first published version; and finally "Civil Disobedience," the more pacific title of the lightly revised final version published a few years after Thoreau's death, generally believed to have been approved if not chosen by him.

At the risk of misrepresenting manifesto as rigorously sequenced argument, the essential ingredients of Thoreau's theory can be boiled down to these. First, the less government, the better. Government is justified only as a necessary expedient. Second, only just governments deserve allegiance. Third, resistance is justified when the state forces one into complicity with its injustice. Fourth, individual conscience is the rightful arbiter of whether and when the injustice is so glaring as to be intolerable. Consent of the governed effectively means "my" consent. My "only obligation . . . is to do what any time I think right." The higher law of conscience trumps the authority of the US Constitution and the principle of majority rule. Indeed, faithfulness to conscience's dictates is a moral imperative more fundamentally important than resolution of the injustice itself. Thoreau heartily seconded Wendell Phillips's affirmation that he "was not born to abolish slavery, but to do right."[6]

Fifth, direct action by persons of conscience is the rightful form of resistance and best guarantor of success. Hence the importance Thoreau attaches to the fanciful-seeming conception of a "majority of one" and the proposition that one man disassociating himself from the corrupt social compact would amount to "the abolition of slavery in America." Whether or not meant literally, these thrusts epitomize Thoreau's almost reflexive anti-institutionalism, including chronic suspicion of the corruptibility of organized reform efforts that he himself sometimes helped further. The closest "Civil Disobedience" comes to envisaging a viable form of collective protest is its passing reference to "a corporation of conscientious men."[7]

Finally, the form of resistance "Civil Disobedience" envisages is nonviolent, ventured in willingness to risk penalty, injury, or incarceration for justice's sake. As *Walden* later puts it, rather than running amok against the state, Thoreau preferred "that society should run 'amok' against me."[8]

Thoreau's call for civil disobedience was warmly welcomed by the mostly Garrisonian antislavery sympathizers who heard and read it, but in Thoreau's lifetime it drew little more than transient local attention and did not become the canonical document it now is until the next century, when Gandhi and then Martin Luther King Jr. credited it with helping inspire their own movements. Significantly, both shared Thoreau's sense of the utmost importance of principled commitment at the individual level, but also with full realization of the insufficiency of stand-alone individualism as the basis for viable collective protest.

In "Civil Disobedience," the conception of "the state" against which resistance might be justified is extremely expansive, indeed tendentiously so, as Thoreau halfway acknowledges. He stretches "state" to encompass not merely the federal government that protected southern slavery under the Constitution and prosecuted the Mexican War but also, and for his purposes especially, the free state

of Massachusetts, which had supplied troops for the war effort. He
included even such unrelated functions as its poll tax, an annual tax
of $1.50 per head on adult males to support town, county, and state
services. Being dunned for that by the local tax collector served as a
ready-to-hand instance of the reach of distant-seeming government
down to the unobtrusive everyday level and the consequent reduction of peaceable citizens, including both victim and arresting offi-
cer, to instruments of the state.

These thrusts give a designedly parochial twist to "Civil
Disobedience" ("I quarrel not with far-off foes")[9] that is accentuated
in Thoreau's next political manifesto, "Slavery in Massachusetts"
(1854), a lecture-essay written and delivered while *Walden* was
in press. It decries state authorities' implementation of the stiff-
ened federal requirements for cooperation in returning escaped
slaves to their legal owners that had been enjoined by the so-called
Compromise of 1850, with the broad support of northern public
opinion. Gone is the concession in "Civil Disobedience" that state
officials might be decent people at heart. Here they are denounced
as supine lackeys from the governor on down. In stark contrast to the
final concession in "Civil Disobedience" that the US Constitution is
a viable fallback for ordinary folk who know no higher law, "Slavery
in Massachusetts" aligns itself squarely with Garrisonian abolitionism in branding the Constitution as a devil's bargain that stands con-
victed by that same higher law. Indeed, the rally at which Thoreau
delivered his address opened with a public burning of a copy of the
Constitution by Garrison himself.

Such thrusts as "Could slavery suggest a more complete servility than some of these journals exhibit?" and "What should con-
cern Massachusetts is not the Nebraska Bill, nor the Fugitive Slave
Bill, but her own slaveholding and servility" direct more outrage
at home-state complicity than at the obnoxious federal legislation
or the plight of the enslaved.[10] Some readers have even questioned
whether Thoreau was so concerned about the institution of slavery
or the welfare of slaves as about slavery as a metaphor for servility in

general, as when *Walden* asserts that being "the slave-driver of your-self" is worse than "the gross but somewhat foreign form of servitude called Negro Slavery."[11]

Thoreauvian hyperbole and metaphor should not be taken so literally, however. The evidence suggests that Thoreau shared little of the prejudice of black inferiority that was then widespread even among abolitionists, including his fellow Transcendentalists Parker and Emerson; and that he assisted escaping slaves with alacrity, consideration, and compassion. What elevated his later apotheosis of John Brown to the topmost place in his personal pantheon of moral heroism was admiration for Brown's unflinching willingness to forfeit his life in order to end slavery.

Thoreau's encomium to Brown as a principled resister of "unjust human laws" to the sacrifice of "bodily life in comparison with ideal things" is wholly consistent with the virtue ethics of "Civil Disobedience."[12] Not so, however, is Thoreau's justification of violent means to achieve worthy ends, a swerve that seems all the greater in light of the earlier work's legacy as a canonical text for non-violent protest movements. Did he contradict himself, then? No and yes. In a sense, later Thoreau simply built upon his earlier calls for principled lawbreaking. Besides, his caveat toward the end of "Civil Disobedience" allows for possible future changes of position: "This, then, is my position at present." Still, the outright justification of Brown's violence ("for once" rifles and revolvers "were employed in a righteous cause") takes Thoreau's earlier rhetorical militancy to a quite different level, just as his exaltation of Brown ("not Old Brown any longer" but "an Angel of Light") far surpasses the praise he ever lavished on anyone else, living or dead.[13]

The fury of Thoreau's denunciations of slavery in the runup to the Civil War increased in tandem with the spread of northern antislavery opposition in reaction to acts of Congress and the judiciary from 1850 onward that strengthened the reach of slaveholding interests in the northern states and the western territories. Abolitionism became more mainstream; calls for disunion and public ritual burnings of the Constitution increased; and New England towns like Concord sent migrants and money to thwart southern settlers' attempted takeover of Kansas as a slave state. Brown first attracted Thoreau's notice during a fund-raising trip to Concord in 1857 that netted pledges from eighteen residents, including $100 from Emerson and $10 from Thoreau's father, the family patriarch. He dined at the Thoreaus, called on the Emersons, and was hosted by a younger townsman, Franklin B. Sanborn, one of the "Secret Six" who planned Brown's 1859 Harpers Ferry raid and in later years wrote memoirs of several Transcendentalists, including Thoreau. Brown's Concord donors may not have known the gory details of the 1856 Pottawatomie Massacre by Brown-led vigilantes or whether their contributions would be used to buy guns, but they could not have failed to be aware that Brown was a guerrilla chief. Thoreau himself had affirmed that "what I most admire now-a-days is not the regular governments but the irregular primitive ones . . . even the free state men in Kansas"—a declaration he repeated after Brown's raid on Harpers Ferry.[14]

Thoreau's legitimation of Brown's violence, then, marked a shift not unique to him but in keeping with the momentum of northern antislavery sentiment. More idiosyncratic was the sheer vehemence of his apotheosis—rivaling if not surpassing all martyrological tributes to the man then or since. The results were predictably controversial. Thoreau's defense amazed those who knew him as a person who generally shunned politics; it provoked charges of fanaticism within the antislavery tribe as well as outside it. But it briefly propelled him to the forefront of ultra-abolitionist advocates. More than two thousand people heard the Boston rendition of his "Plea for Captain John Brown"—by far his largest audience ever.[15] It took the lead position in abolitionist James Redpath's 1860 *Echoes of Harper's Ferry*, ahead of selections by Phillips, Emerson, and Parker. His "Last Days of John Brown," the third of his three Brown eulogies, was delivered in absentia by one of Brown's associates at a memorial graveside service on July 4, 1860. Its parting shot ("He is more alive than ever he was") was one of the first all-out predictions of Brown's unstoppable charismatic power, which at least in a small way Thoreau himself helped make possible.[16]

For Thoreau to idealize Brown as acting from conscience rather than contingency was thus itself at least partly a contingent result of the growing receptivity among northern abolitionists to violent methods of resisting state-sanctioned slavery that eventually overtook even Garrison. That no doubt also reinforced the personal partiality Thoreau clearly also felt for Brown as something of a kindred spirit: a new Englander "by descent and birth," a fellow surveyor, assertive in conviction, emphatic in expression, who hated profanity, "a man of Spartan habits" who was selective and demanding in his choice of associates.[17] All these were qualities Emerson praised in Thoreau after his death a few years later.

Of the force of these influences, if influences they were, Thoreau himself may not have been more than partially aware. Be that as it may, it is noteworthy that his efforts as righteous champion subsided soon after Brown's death, almost as if a spell had been broken. That too was broadly typical of Thoreau's political activism. His wariness at getting embroiled in hot-button public issues was chronic; his periods of intense engagement were sporadic; and his sense of relief at returning to what he never ceased to consider his primary pursuits was palpable. Hence the flourish of ending the incarceration narrative in "Civil Disobedience" with his breakaway to the hills to captain a huckleberry party and the abrupt shift at the end of "Slavery in Massachusetts" from righteous wrath to the consolation of discovering a beautiful water lily on a spring walk. The symbol of purity springing up in slime proves that "Nature has been partner to no Missouri Compromise," that even "slavery and servility" may inspire a regeneration of the human spirit once they're buried and reduced to manure.[18]

These touchstone scenes of nature immersion as antidote to politics point to more sweeping questions about the place of the "political" for Thoreau—including what should count as the "political"—that extend far beyond the handful of lecture-essays centering on explicitly political issues. They witness to a settled determination to minimize potentially compromising social entanglements, however worthy. Often, as here, they invoke reconnection with "Nature" as counter-norm and standard of value that in turn suggests the difficulty of banishing the social from view however much one might wish. Indeed, it is quite likely that Thoreau was much more aware of current events than his writing usually acknowledges, that his mention of strolling "every day or two" into town from his Walden retreat "to hear some of the gossip which is incessantly going on there" should be taken more seriously than the breezily satirical tone implies. Though one can only speculate, the scattered *Journal* expressions of relief that foraging for plants and berries "drives Kansas out of your head" or the occasional strictures on current events in letters to family and friends seem tips of an iceberg—or volcano—of which he chose mostly not to speak.[19]

How, then, to define such a stance? Where does one place Thoreau on, or off, the map of political theory and/or the history of political thought? The answer hinges perhaps most crucially on how if at all "can a stance towards the world that is based on conscience be called 'political,'" as political theorist Nancy Armstrong observed shortly after Thoreau's political ideas had begun to attract more than passing attention from philosophers in the 1970s.[20] Until then, with scattered exceptions the mantle of Thoreau's ultra-individualism had been claimed chiefly by opposite political fringe groups: anarchists and libertarians, with both Emma Goldman and the John Birch Society enlisting Thoreau as forebear.

The issue remains a matter of debate. Broadly speaking, the case for Thoreau's relevance as a political thinker is usually seen as resting on the importance attached to individual self-realization by democratic theory, especially US democratic theory, in terms of which the relation between individual and state is often held to be at least incipiently adversarial. From this standpoint, Thoreau's avowals of disengagement from the polis; his denigration of political and civic institutions as a lesser order of reality compromising to the demands of conscience and personal integrity; and even his declarations of war with or secession from the state might be seen as contributions to a robustly multistranded tradition of democratic dissent.

Pushed beyond a certain point, however, this line of argument can seem to preempt Thoreau by syllogistic fiat, as an inexorable deduction from the premise that "individuality's meaning is not fully disclosed until it is indissociably connected to democracy." Against this, it has been argued no less forcibly that Thoreau's will to dissociate himself from politics must be taken seriously, that he sought to depoliticize "the political relations of life to accommodate his moral sensibility."[21] Political theorist Jonathan McKenzie presses this view to the limit in characterizing Thoreau as a neo-Stoic moralist at heart for whom entanglement in public affairs was an irritating, even morally hazardous, distraction from the crucial work of self-fashioning. McKenzie even goes so far as to conceive both Thoreau's sporadic activism and the political manifestoes from "Civil Disobedience" onward as "momentary interludes" that witness to "failures to properly craft and care for an insulated self." This assessment gives a more sophisticated and positive spin to older-style dismissals by Hannah Arendt and others of Thoreau's appeals to conscience as inherently "unpolitical."[22]

The truth of the matter surely falls somewhere between the extremes of these divergent claims. Yes, the arenas of political thought and action, however expansively one defines the political, were lesser priorities for Thoreau in principle than moral rectitude and moral improvement, and incontestably he did see the former as potentially compromising to the latter. Equally incontestable, though, is the case for an always at least incipiently or residually political Thoreau. For the most part, that political Thoreau expresses himself negatively by critiques of institutional arrangements in every sphere—social, political, religious, scientific, literary—that seek to distance himself as far as possible from the institution in question. But no small part of what animates such critique in the first place is the will to instruct his listeners about how to live within society as well as against it, however much he leavens his advice-giving with mock-didactic drollery. Witness *Walden's* opening assertions that the book began in answer to questions put by his townsmen and is offered as a testament to neighbors, "poor students," and fellow New Englanders generally. On such grounds, as Stanley Cavell suggests, *Walden* qualifies as, "among other things, a tract of political educa-tion, education for membership in the polis."[23] And an American polis to boot, insofar as the ingredients from which Thoreau fash-ions his recipe for successful coexistence are also distinctive to US-style democratic ideology: such as the dignity of the free-standing individual, limited government, and suspicion of established institu-tions and hierarchies.

Thoreau's own last word on the subject is "Life without Principle," a philippic on society-as-usual's threat to individual personhood delivered as a lyceum lecture from 1854 onward but continuously revised down to the last weeks of his life. Next to his more overtly political writings, it sounds crotchety rather than impassioned, and anticlimactic in its reprise of *Walden's* satire on moneygrubbing mate-rialism without *Walden's* fresh-start counternarrative. Irritability without uplift, as it were. But that is what makes it relevant here. On the one hand, it attests that sociopolitical pathologies preoccupied Thoreau on an ongoing basis, not just episodically. Likewise, the persona appears here in citizen's rather than hermit's guise as the honest surveyor vexed by profit-hungry landowner-employers; nor does he offer the alternative of pastoral retreat from the arena. To that extent, "Life without Principle" confirms the thesis of a Thoreau who understood himself, like it or not, as a disaffected citizen of a republic of unfulfilled promise. The rhetorical question with which it culminates nails the core issue: "What is the value of any political freedom, but as a means to moral freedom?"[24]

Thoreau's answer lacks the pungency of the manifestoes, ener-gized as they are by specific occasions that goaded him to a concen-trated outrage absent here. It is instructive, however, in dramatizing the limits of Thoreau's investment in political issues. After denouncing America's "exclusive devotion to trade and commerce" for the nth time, the essay lurches to the conclusion that politics is a necessary although inferior organ of the body social, "the gizzard of society," which ought to function routinely and subliminally, leaving the average citizen blessedly unaware of its workings.[25] Political consciousness, then, is a kind of moral dyspepsia begotten on the unwilling individual by derangement of the state. It is hard to imagine a more grudging acknowledgment of the claims of the political or a more decisive affirmation of the inherent superiority of moral aspiration to political engagement.

As such, Thoreau's last word about politics also suggests that "Civil Disobedience" was more faithful overall than were the later manifestoes to his deepest convictions, in its clear preference for countering injustice through passive resistance rather than aggression: not through open but "quiet" war, as the essay puts it. If so, that should cheer the majority of Thoreauvians who prefer the canonical image of the patron saint of nonviolent protest to the incendiary Thoreau of "Slavery in Massachusetts" and especially of "A Plea for Captain John Brown." Yet those too remain crucial portions of his political writing: memorable intrinsically and historically as landmark expressions of rising antislavery militancy; as witnesses to Thoreau's emergence, belated and brief as it was, as a front-rank partisan; and as proof positive that for Thoreau himself, if not for posterity, the philosophy of nonviolent protest laid out on "Civil Disobedience" was indeed an interim report rather than a final resting place.

Chapter 7

Matters of Faith

Over the years, Thoreau's life and writings have become canonical in a sense more literal than what is usually meant by a "canonical" figure in the history of literature or philosophy or science. No one speaks of Saint Mark (Twain), Saint Ernest (Hemingway), Saint Charles (Darwin), or Saint Immanuel (Kant). But Thoreau has become invested, in some quarters anyhow, with an image of secular sainthood. This process started as early as his Walden years, with his friend Ellery Channing's poetic evocation of Thoreau as a holy hermit piously dwelling in his Walden retreat. Tributes to Thoreau as the voice of moral or spiritual or environmental conscience have continued down to the present, often leavened by gentle irony toward his crotchets or blind spots to make the homage more credible. In his "Letter to Thoreau" at the start of his *The Future of Life*, for example, biologist E. O. Wilson praises Thoreau as "the founding saint of the conservation movement," then proceeds to itemize his limitations as a naturalist.[1] Hundreds of homage-tributes of the "my Thoreau" variety line the pages of the *Thoreau Society Bulletin* (1941–). Among the fruits of the outpouring of Thoreauviana on the bicentennial of his birth in 2017 was a collection tellingly titled *What Would Henry Do?*

Today, Thoreau-centric sermons are often delivered from liberal Protestant pulpits. (I have heard several and even given one myself.) Lecturers on the literary or scientific or political Thoreau who venture beyond their academic cloisters to hold forth before mixed audiences on Thoreau the writer or scientist or activist should be prepared to be told, as I have, that they have missed the boat entirely: that Thoreau was essentially a yogi.

Reverence for Thoreau, whether fervently or ironically expressed, as a species of holy man, oracle, guru, life companion, and guide has mainly been the work of his posterity. But it would not have happened if he had not lived as he did, thought as he did, and written as he did. With one side of his being, Thoreau was clearly a quester after ultimates—of spiritual, moral, and natural truth—with a strong perfectionist aspiration and, for a time at least, also a pronounced mystical bent. His life and writing reveal at least four distinctive but overlapping manifestations of that aspiration. A review of these should also explain how Thoreau, consciously or unconsciously, helped inspire his own apotheosis, to the satisfaction of his admirers and the disgruntlement of his detractors.

The most obvious of the four manifestations might be called Thoreau the Exhorter. This is the Thoreau who pronounces emphatic judgment on matters of belief, value, and conduct. In this he was by no means alone among leading writers of his day. The nineteenth century was the heyday of the Victorian sage, and Thoreau hoped to be one of the sages. The link between writerly and prophetic calling was then thought to be more intimate than for any era since the era of ancient bardic poetry. Serious-minded literati felt called to wrestle with fundamental questions of religion, morality, and social justice. A series of Anglo-American poets from William Blake to Walt Whitman saw themselves as conduits of revelation. Shelley declared that poets were "the unacknowledged legislators of the world." Whitman hoped that *Leaves of Grass* might be a "New Bible."[2] A number of writers were acclaimed as secular prophets: Carlyle, Emerson, Margaret Fuller, Harriet Beecher Stowe, Matthew Arnold, John Ruskin, and others. The high seriousness of the leading novelists of the day refuted the old stereotype of the inherent frivolity of the genre. All this was part of a much broader surge of moral and spiritual exhortation at the grassroots level in such popular genres as slave narrative, temperance fiction, sectarian tracts, and self-help literature of all kinds, some of it written by card-carrying clerics but most not.

This prophetic turn was driven by a mix of positive and negative energies that followed from the erosion of traditional certitudes of morality and religion. Emerson's transformation from minister to inspirational writer and speaker was a case in point. Thoreau, inheriting the changing landscape that Emerson and other Transcendentalist elders had helped to shape, was more stridently iconoclastic. Whatever scant attachment he ever had to religious observances soon evaporated: respect for ministers, churchgoing, saying grace at meals. While still in his early twenties he made an elaborate show of resigning his membership in the local parish, and he remained thereafter an outspoken critic of conventional religion, more unsparingly so than Emerson, who continued to attend church, preach occasionally, and garb himself in clerical black when lecturing to lyceum audiences.

Thoreau preferred a practical workingman's corduroy outfit that led some to mistake him for the laborer he sometimes was. But sententiousness ran as strong in him as in his mentor. In his social reform essays a preacherly voice dominates, as in "Life without Principle," "Slavery in Massachusetts," and his eulogies to John Brown. Nowhere is this voice more emphatic, however, than in his chastisements of the religious status quo. Thoreau's writing bristles with indignant putdowns of "factitious piety like stale gingerbread," unctuous "ministers who spoke of God as if they enjoyed a monopoly of the subject," worshipers whose zombie-like conventionalism proved "no infidelity so great as that which prays and keeps the Sabbath." He had a chip-on-shoulder penchant for cutting Judeo-Christianity down to size by harping on Jesus's limitations of character ("his thoughts were all directed to another world") and the inferiority of Jehovah to Jove ("more absolute and unapproachable, but hardly more divine").[3] Running throughout his *Journal* entries for Sunday mornings is a vein of satire on the dutiful pieties of New

Englanders as essentially the same as that of Roman peasantry or Pacific Islanders.

When reviewers denounced Thoreau's infidelity and editors rejected or bowdlerized his irreverent prose, more often than not it reinforced his disdain and his pertinacity. After one magazine editor irked him by deleting from one manuscript his remark that Catholicism might be better "if the priest were quite omitted,"[4] Thoreau proceeded to offer the same party a longer project with a more extended sequence of limit-bumping satire—with the predictable result that the series was summarily quashed.

Such asperity implied freethinking heterodoxy rather than downright atheism. Like many who outgrow a conventional religious upbringing, Thoreau gave up on church before he gave up on God, if indeed he ever did. He was an early exemplar of the persuasion today called "spiritual but not religious" that many claim holds for most Americans: resolutely antisectarian, but no less resolutely a seeker of truth with a capital *T*. Even as he extricated himself from the residues of conventional theism, he continued to be drawn by the sense of an accessible higher power, whether in nature or in the inner illuminations of one's spirit; and by the force of those experiences he believed himself to have felt. His flippancy toward the "Christian fable" masked a lasting interest in the foundational sacred texts of world religions generally as repositories of timeless truth—almost the only "collective expression of tradition for which he held any real regard."[5] An early case in point was his oversight of the "Ethnical Scriptures" series for *The Dial*: snippets of wisdom and anecdote culled from French translations of ancient Hindu, Confucian, Buddhist, and Islamic sources. At one point, Thoreau even floated the idea of a collection of "Scriptures or Sacred Writings of the several nations" as a means "to liberalize the faith of men," a "Book of Books" that its missionaries might "carry to the uttermost parts of the earth."[6]

In such ways, he advanced Transcendentalism's religious agenda as vigorously as the credentialed clerics like Emerson who comprised the largest fraction of the movement's male nucleus. All had absorbed, whether directly or by osmosis as Thoreau did, the premises of the Higher Criticism imported by American liberal theologians from Germany a generation before, according to which they reconceived the Bible in the light of comparative mythology. In practice that meant, on the one hand, denying its literal truth and subjecting it to interpretive analysis like any literary text and, on the other, openness to other world religions as legitimate sources of inspiration. After Thoreau's death, other Transcendentalists including Emerson took the vision further in such ventures as the interfaith Free Religious Association.

Thoreau himself was much less interested in generating ecumenical movements than in channeling the energies of the new cosmopolitan spirituality into his life and writing. The prospect of a more expansive set of pathways to primal wisdom especially excited him. That was the spiritual face of the back-to-origins thrusts in *A Week* and *Walden*: their enthusiasm for the aboriginal phases of both Native and settler culture, for returning to the fundamentals of economic subsistence, and for an idealized classical antiquity. In both books, especially *Walden*, Thoreau gives his prose a scriptural tang by injections of parables and pronouncements from the Vedas, Confucius, Mencius, Laozi, and classical Indic and Persian literature and by selective enlistment of Christian texts and tropes ("Walden was dead and is alive again"). The effect is reinforced by the proverb-laden idiom of the moral essay from Seneca to Bacon onward that he had long since internalized: "the wisest have ever lived a more simple and meager life," "no odor as bad as that which arises from goodness tainted," "a man sits as many risks as he runs." In such ways, memoir metamorphoses into testament.[7]

In Thoreau's reform writing, the tone of authoritative Thus-saith-the-Lord pronouncement is even more insistent, torquing lecture-essay into homily, as in "Under a government which imprisons any unjustly, the true place for a just man is also a prison" ("Civil Disobedience"); "Read not the Times, Read the Eternities" ("Life without Principle"); and the exhortation to obey not the nation's Constitution but the divine: "that eternal and only just CONSTITU-TION which He, and not any Jefferson or Adams, has written in your being" ("Slavery in Massachusetts").[8]

Thoreau did not feel called to play prophet except intermit-tently, however. Here he differed from the literati of his day whose work interested him most: Carlyle, Emerson, and Whitman. His high hopes for human potential were more often directed toward personal perfection than the reformation of humanity at large, and that aspiration, as time went on, was complicated by a redirection of mental energies from self-examination toward fascinated contem-plation of the workings of the natural world.

In Thoreau's writing, *Walden* marks the ascendancy of Thoreau the Seeker and the emergence of Thoreau the Apostle of Nature. Not that the didactic impulse in him has by any means died out here. On the contrary, *Walden* was Thoreau's most concerted attempt to write secular scripture—a life-changing testimony with the depth and density of the ancient moral and religious classics. ("How many a man has dated a new era in his life from the reading of a book," declares one telling aside.) But the temptation to preach runs up against Thoreau's principled aversion to bullying pontification, as well as an ingrained skepticism about the efficacy of preaching that reverberates through the text in a series of wryly self-undermining scenes, from the wistful to the hilarious, that confess the quixotism of his evangelizing attempts. He cannot coax his affable unlettered French Canadian woodsman friend "to take the spiritual view of things."[9] He utterly fails to convert the Irish immigrant laborer John Field to his voluntary simplicity regime. Sometimes he cannot even follow his own advice, as when, after pressing a neo-Hindu gospel of asceticism to the limit in "Higher Laws," he immediately lets himself be tempted away from his contemplative exercises by the lure of fish-ing, a pursuit he had just renounced.

Such derailments of the didactic momentum push back against the excesses of self-discipline, uncomfortably like those he chided in his townsmen, to which he knew himself to be prone even as he sought to "undistract himself" from conventional pursuits.[10] They also point to more fundamental shifts in his thinking during the decade between the Walden experience itself and the book's completion.

Thoreau's removal to Walden had unleashed a burst of elation that lasted nearly the whole first summer. He had turned a new page in life. He had felt himself translated into the mythic realms he had dreamed about for years: into the company of Hector and Ulysses, somehow "favored by the Gods" and "especially guided and guarded." Others with whom he crossed paths seemed transfigured too. "Even the tired laborers I meet on the road, I really meet as traveling Gods." Intimations of the infinite potential and inherent divinity of the human shimmer throughout *Walden*, as in "every man is the lord of a realm" larger than imperial Russia and "a tide rises and falls behind every man which can float the British Empire like a chip"; or when the sight of a rainbow seems a message from "my good Genius" of his own special chosenness.[11]

Walden registers that sense of exaltation at the ground level of the plot in hundreds of vignettes that showcase the author-protagonist trying to live every act deliberately: his daily ritual bath, baking bread or planting beans as the ancients did, declining the gift of a doormat to "avoid the beginnings of evil," even in his all-morning do-nothing doorstep "revery" ("I realized what the Orientals mean by contemplation and the forsaking of works"). More than anywhere else in Thoreau's writings except for his *Journal*, *Walden* portrays its actor in the process of self-consciously enacting his own script stage by stage, feeling his way as he goes; lapsing and willfully veering from it along the way, but in the long run progressing well enough to bear out the conclusion that the experience yielded paradigmatically transformative results. "If one advances confidently in the direction of his dreams, and endeavors to live the life which he has imagined," Thoreau sums up, "he will meet with a success unexpected in common hours."[12]

This, then, is the second way in which Thoreau's writings prepared the way for his future sainthood: by casting Thoreauvian doctrine into the soul-saga of a seeker all the more potentially appealing for the fusion of proffered model and warts-and-bumps fallibility. After all, from such fusions have many of the lives of officially certified saints also been fashioned, Augustine for instance. No wonder Thoreau found himself drawn to Whitman's *Leaves of Grass*, which does the same thing more extravagantly, despite Thoreau's prudish recoil from the more risqué passages in which it seemed to him "as if the beasts spoke."[13] By the end of *Walden*, the Thoreauvian persona will have fixed itself in the sympathetic reader's mind as a dedicated practitioner if not a master of all the arts of living it commends: how to build, plaster, furnish, cook, eat, drink, sleep, wake, dress, wash, read, till, fish, boat, meditate, listen, travel, self-examine, balance society and solitude, interact with nature, thrive cheerfully in winter, enjoy every day, know when to move on to the next life-stage. This flesh-and-blood depiction of self as exemplary Seeker makes for a much more compelling self-dramatization than Thoreau the Exhorter. This especially is the Thoreau around whom posterity's vision of Saint Henry has been built. This especially is the Thoreau who has inspired thousands of pilgrimages to Walden Pond. This is the Thoreau who has inspired the many life-experiments in simplicity and dissent that claim his precedent, like one worshipful back-to-the-land memoir that opens, "We went to the wilderness because 100 years ago a man wrote a book."[14] This is the Thoreau who has drawn many more to *Walden* as a vade mecum.

Walden's self-transforming impetus tallies with the core doctrine of the already-published "Civil Disobedience" insofar as voluntary simplicity and piloting by one's inner compass are keys to both. With this in mind, Thoreau scholar Alda Balthrop-Lewis proposes "political asceticism" as a master term for his underlying spiritual stance.[15] Such was his homeopathic remedy for the pseudo-asceticisms that he satirized in conventionally ambitious neighbors who overburdened themselves with goods and debt to get ahead, in mill girls

Walden Pond in the 1890s, a view looking southwest from Thoreau's house site sixty years after his sojourn there and a quarter-century after Thoreauvian pilgrimages to Walden had begun. The cairn of votive stones is the work of early pilgrims. Photograph by A. W. Hosmer, as reprinted in Annie Russell Marble, *Thoreau: His Home, Friends, and Books* (New York: Crowell, 1902). *Courtesy of Walden Woods Project.*

affixed to their workstations, in the straitened existences of the marginal inhabitants who peopled Walden's woods before him.

The practice of voluntary simplicity in a space apart that *Walden* dramatizes also meant, however, deep immersion in that environment as well as contending against the regime disowned. Physical nature, not just the idea of the thing, looms up as the crucial spirit-cleanser and catalyst for the persona's passage from routine to mindfully disencumbered living ("Let us spend one day as deliberately as Nature").[16]

Here *Walden* registers the shift that had been taking place during its time of composition in the author's attention from self to the surrounding woods-world. When Thoreau started the book, he was still seeking his vocational path. By the time he completed it, he had settled the matter and reached a point when his transactions with the natural world, as student and experiencer, had become a more important, or at least more overt, preoccupation than his own moral and spiritual condition. Not that the latter ceased to matter intensely to him, nor—especially at moments of public crisis—did the many social injustices of the day, slavery chief among them. But increasingly he looked to responsive attention to the workings, health, and beauty of the natural world as a steadying, nurturing force for himself personally and as a benchmark for social health and pathology.

Initially there was something mystical in his attraction to nature, a pantheistic element. Again and again it surfaces in *Walden*. At such moments, the book seems to be striving to make good on the credo he jotted down in his journal midway through the writing of it: "My profession is to be always on the alert to find God in nature." As *Walden* unfolds, the pond looms up not only as its geographical center and all-seasons resort of pleasure and fascination, but also as a numinous presence, a benign equivalent of the white whale in Melville's *Moby-Dick*. Walden becomes a personified character, agent, partaker in the narrative: a companion, a soulmate, a symbol of purity to which the speaker aspires and even apostrophizes as a deific presence into with which he feels himself at times absorbed ("I am its stony shore"). The sweep of the narrative reinforces the sense of the immanence of the holy conferred upon one who lives through the seasonal cycle faithfully practicing "the discipline of looking always at what is to be seen."[17] The process culminates in the exultation of spring bursting forth like the Christian resurrection and the return of the classical Golden Age combined. Along the way, Thoreau's repeated invocations of animals, birds, and trees of the vicinity as companions give flesh to Emerson's theory of "an occult relation between the man and the vegetable."[18]

Yet *Walden*'s dramatization of human entanglement in the natural also has a distinctly materialist dimension that runs counter to its mystical propensities even as it gestures toward them, as when the narrator exclaims: "Shall I not have intelligence with the earth? Am I not partly leaves and vegetable mould itself?" The second question brings the mysticism of the first literally down to earth. Likewise, *Walden's* springtime fantasia of the railroad sandbank at the pond's edge thawing into simulacra of every conceivable human body part depicts the scene both ethereally, as "the laboratory of the Artist who made the world and me," and earthily, likening "the silicious matter which the water deposits" to "the bony system."[19]

Thoreau's "terrenial turn," as biographer Laura Dassow Walls calls it,[20] becomes especially salient in the second half of *Walden* from "The Ponds" onward, where the bulk of the late additions were made, fleshing out the barebones environmental detail of the early drafts with elaboration of the geology of Walden and nearby sister ponds, its physical changes over time and through the seasons, and the flora and fauna of the locale. As the seasons roll on, the memoirist begins to modulate from instructor-exemplar of essential truths of living to dramatizer-guardian of the local wildlands.

This unstable synthesis of nature mysticism and empirical sturdiness is the third way in which Thoreau's writing lends itself to later apotheosis: Thoreau the Apostle of Nature. This avatar has both a mystical and a down-to-earth side: Thoreau as Green Man, or Patron Saint of Environmentalism. Take your pick, or choose both if the spirit moves.

During Thoreau's last half-dozen years, the sense of the numinous largely fades from his writing, as does his interest in literary scripturalism. In the mid-1850s, he was thrilled to receive a British friend's munificent gift of several dozen valuable translations of Sanskrit classics, which instantly became the cornerstone of his library, he declared in an effusive thank-you letter. But most of them he had read before, and he rarely dipped into them again. Likewise, with scattered exceptions neither his later *Journal* nor his later books record experiences that match the moments of ecstasy one finds in a number of the early poems, the early Walden *Journal*, "Ktaadn," and portions of his first two books. Rarely do we encounter such grand assertions of direct connectedness with the divine as "God himself culminates in the present moment" and "Man flows at once to

God when the channel of purity is open."[21] The "Chesuncook" and "Allegash and East Branch" portions of *The Maine Woods, Cape Cod,* "Dispersion of Seeds," and "Wild Fruits" are solidly earthbound by contrast.

This shift has a melancholy aspect that readers familiar with Wordsworthian-style laments about the fading of visionary gleam after youth will easily recognize. As his experiences of spontaneous illumination diminished, Thoreau had to confess that only "in the rarest moments" did he feel the stirrings of "some divinity" within; that "99/100ths of our lives we are mere hedgers & ditchers." Not long after leaving Walden, in fact, he warned an admirer that he saw himself rising to the plane of "a yogin" only "at rare intervals." When another wrote to him hopefully about some day meeting the author of *Walden,* Thoreau replied that the best of him was in his books and "I am not worth seeing personally—the stuttering, blundering, clod-hopper that I am."[22]

Such ruefulness is hardly the whole story, however, not even the main story. Not only did Thoreau's mental energies continue unabated until his last illness, but the image of a fully de-Transcendentalized Thoreau who cast the residues of theism and pantheism behind him can be seen, has been seen, and at least up to a point certainly should be seen as a progression rather than a decline—a fulfillment more complete. In the later *Journal,* the mood swings and surges of restless striving diminish in proportion to the sense of deepening satisfaction at being grounded in the place where he is, for all its limitations, for all his own imperfections.

Especially in recent years some have mounted strong arguments to the effect that this late Thoreau was always at least incipiently the essential Thoreau: that he was always more disposed than Emerson or other Transcendentalist confreres toward empiricism, or more precisely to a conception of nature and humankind as networked within ongoing nonteleological processes entirely material in nature. "Vitalistic materialism," Thoreau scholar Branka Arsić terms it: a postpantheism shorn of mystical residues.[23]

This way of thinking has the attraction of making Thoreau more appealingly modern while at the same time highlighting some of his more long-standing proclivities. Not only does it speak to the momentum of Thoreau's later thought as his habits of empirical observation took increasing hold. From his youth onward, from "Sic Vita" to *Cape Cod* and "Autumnal Tints," moreover, a kind of neo-Stoic fatalism with much more ancient roots often suffuses his musings about death, loss, and the fragility of human life and relationships measured against the force of natural process, such that acceptance of the former often seems inseparable from affirmation of the latter.

That said, the notion of Thoreau as a species of materialist thinker must also confront several obstacles. For one thing, mystical flareups do recur in late Thoreau, as in an often-cited passage from "Chesuncook" in which he imagines a pine tree towering over him in the afterlife. The passage prompted an angry outburst from Thoreau when his cautious editor deleted it as heretical. Then too, he clearly continued to think of moral law in absolute terms and nature (often with a capital *N*) as an ethical norm: a reproach to human moral lapse—personal, social, political. Emerson's dictum that Nature is "a fixed point whereby we may measure our departure" remained hardwired in Thoreau's psychic makeup.[24]

Indeed, the very commitment to empirical research that led him away from nature mysticism seems also to have been reinforced by a secularized version of natural piety: the sense that physical nature operates according to laws, however random they may seem, on which the welfare of persons and societies depend. This assumption seems implicit in the lower-key tropes in Thoreau's late natural history writings that supersede the earlier mystical-poetic ones, such as the imaginary "Patent Office at the seat of the government of the universe" in "Dispersion of Seeds" that distributes seeds around the globe, with squirrels and other creatures acting as the government's quasi-personified agents, wiser than the farmers who curse them.[25] The underlying claim here is basically identical to *Walden*'s "Next to us the grandest laws are continually being executed."[26] Thoreau's late-life fieldwork remained "essentially reverential" in involving "a continual testing of his faith in a vital, harmonious, and evolving cosmos, and a persistent attempt to reclaim his own place in it."[27]

Nor did Thoreau cease to resort to more conventional God-talk when it suited him, as in his hagiography of John Brown. Running throughout his work is a kind of pop-up theism, as in casual references to "the Author of the Universe" or "the greater Benefactor and Intelligence that stands over me the human insect."[28] Over time, however, "God" became rather a placeholder for the property of the Absolute in morals or nature that Thoreau seems to have been quite content to leave undefined. Perhaps the closest he ever came to explaining what he meant by God was an enigmatic passage in an 1850 letter advising a disciple to "let *God* alone." "It is not when I am going to meet him," he adds, "but when I am just turning away and leaving him alone, that I discover that God is. I say God. I am not sure that that is the name."[29]

Altogether, though the matter is bound to remain debatable, Thoreau's spiritual leanings seem to have followed an arc from iconoclastic theism toward pantheism toward materialism that at every stage remained exploratory, without crystallizing into a settled position and without the prior stage or stages altogether disappearing before the next. What is more certain is that by his early thirties if not before he had taken his own advice and largely bracketed subjects like the nature of God, afterlife, and personal immortality as superfluous to the task of living rightly and coming into right relation with the natural world around him.

Thoreau's bond to the Concord landscape in later years rarely became routine. Familiarity bred not contempt but an ever-deepening contentment. Except when on duty as surveyor, each semiredundant sortie seemed a challenge to see afresh. That in turn quickened his alertness to the minute, ever-shifting phenomena from which his accounts of seed dispersion and fruitage were woven and with it his feelings "akin to reverence" for every swamp, rock, animal, stone, tree. "The more thrilling, wonderful, divine objects I behold in a day, the more expanded & immortal I become," one such *Journal* entry affirms.[30] Such experiences seem not so much mystical or pantheistic as eco-phenomenological: a felt extension of mind/body triggered by sensuous contact.

Flash forward now to Thoreau's final eighteen-month decline after the bronchitis he contracted in December 1860 reactivated the tuberculosis that had plagued him and others in his family for years. Though understandably frustrated by increasing debility and confinement, by all accounts Thoreau faced the end with remarkable equanimity. He died peacefully, indeed serenely, among caring family and attentive friends and neighbors, with no sign of vexation that his life had been cut short except for his anxiety to get as many of his nearly finished manuscripts as possible off to his publisher.

In this we see a final avatar of Thoreauvian sainthood, which like the third has two faces. One, assiduously curated by his sister and primary caregiver Sophia, is Thoreau as exemplar of the "good death" that pious middle-class nineteenth-century Protestant culture longed for, in defiance of the epidemiological realities of terminal tuberculosis, a wasting disease that devours the lungs from the inside out. "Henry accepts this dispensation," she wrote, "with such childlike trust and is so happy that I feel as if he were being translated rather than dying in the way of most mortals."[31] Though such affirmations must be discounted as Victorian consolation rhetoric aimed at propping up family and friends, they are supported by a range of eyewitnesses, among them Thoreau's ex-jailer Sam Staples, who told Emerson that he "never saw a man dying with so much pleasure & peace."[32] Here the more timebound face of model Victorian dying montages into the more exalted image of the death of the exemplary philosopher-sage: alert, wise, and unperturbed to the last. This is the Thoreau who is said to have replied to an acquaintance's question if he was able to peer into futurity: "One world at a time." Or to the aunt who asked if he had made his peace with God: "I did not know we had ever quarrelled."[33] This Socrates-Thoreau image was doubtless also cosmeticized, yet it was consistent with the man who had held that illness is a state to be savored as much as health and that dying is as natural as living; with the man who never seems to have lamented the untimeliness of his death, however much his admirers did.

* * *

"Saints should always be judged guilty until they are proved innocent"—so begins George Orwell's essay on Gandhi.[34] So too with Thoreau, maybe. The contours of his inner spiritual life are elusive, with an ad hoc character to their unfolding that becomes harder to trace as his inner thrashings diminished and therewith the need to ponder them even to himself. The phases of possible sainthood reviewed here partly line up, partly jostle against each other—a caution against engraving any of them in stone. Those that do may be misled, sometimes spectacularly, as with the rudderless young adventurer Christopher McCandless, who ventured into the Alaska wilderness in the 1990s woefully unprepared and was found dead with this sentence (among others) highlighted in his copy of *Walden*: "No man ever followed his genius till it misled him."[35] If one looks to Thoreau, however, not as an oracle but as a stimulus to see and be beyond the ordinary and to maintain that alertness in the face of temptation to lapse into routine and banality, then it becomes far more understandable that his life story and his writing should have touched so many.

NOTES

Abbreviations

CD Thoreau, "Civil Disobedience" (aka "Resistance to Civil Government"), in *Reform Papers*. Ed. Wendell Glick. Princeton, NJ: Princeton University Press, 1973. Quotations are from this standard edition of Thoreau's collected works, even though it uses the title of the essay's first (1849) printing rather than the much better-known title of the slightly revised version published a few years after Thoreau's death that most scholars agree he must have approved if not invented.

J Thoreau, *Journal*. 8 vols. to date of a projected 16. Ed. John Broderick et al. Princeton NJ: Princeton University Press, 1981–. Thoreau's punctuation is occasionally regularized for the sake of readability.

J1906 *The Journal of Henry David Thoreau*. 14 vols. Ed. Bradford Torrey and Francis H. Allen. Boston: Houghton Mifflin, 1906. Now being superseded by J. Quotations checked for accuracy against the authoritative online edition of Thoreau's journal: http://thoreau.library.ucsb.edu/writings_journals.html.

Wa Thoreau, *Walden, or Life in the Woods*. Ed. J. Lyndon Shanley. Princeton, NJ: Princeton University Press, 1971.

Chapter 1

1. Edward Abbey, "Down the River with Henry Thoreau," in *Slumgullion Stew: An Edward Abbey Reader* (New York: Dutton, 1984), 195.

2. *Wa* 90.

3. *Wa* 90, 97, 8.

4. Virginia Woolf, "Thoreau," in *Books and Portraits: Some Further Selections from the Literary and Biographical Writings of Virginia Woolf* (London: Hogarth Press, 1977), 75.

5. *Wa* 88–89.

6. *Wa* 232.

7. *J* 1:381, 172, 494.

8. Ralph Waldo Emerson, "Concord Hymn," in *The Collected Works of Ralph Waldo Emerson*, vol. 9: *Poems: A Variorum Edition*, ed. Albert von Frank (Cambridge, MA: Harvard University Press, 2011), 307.

9. Robert A. Gross, *The Transcendentalists and Their World* (New York: Farrar, Straus and Giroux, 2021), 595.

10. *J* 2:374.

11. *Wa* 327.

12. Thoreau, "Walking," in *Excursions*, ed. Joseph J. Moldenhauer (Princeton, NJ: Princeton University Press, 2007), 191.

13. Ibid., 190–191.

14. Ibid., 195–197, 202.

15. Ibid., 206, 216.

16. *J* 3:319.

17. Emerson, "Thoreau," in *Collected Works of RWE*, vol. 10: *Uncollected Prose Writings*, ed. Ronald A. Bosco and Joel Myerson (Cambridge, MA: Harvard University Press, 2013), 416.

18. *The Correspondence of Henry D. Thoreau*, ed. Robert N. Hudspeth, 3 vols. (2 vols. published to date) (Princeton, NJ: Princeton University Press, 2013), 1:313.

19. *J1906* 9:337, 146. For more on this issue, see Cristin Ellis, "On Thoreau's Ecoerotics," in *Dispersion: Thoreau and Vegetal Thought*, ed. Branka Arsić (New York: Bloomsbury, 2021), 165–188.

20. *J* 5:212.

Chapter 2

1. Henry S. Salt, *Life of Henry David Thoreau* (London: Richard Bentley & Son, 1890).

2. *Wa* 10.

3. *Wa* 98.

4. *Wa* 69.

5. *CD* 89.

6. *Wa* 205–206, 74.

7. *Wa* 329, 23, 74, 40, 331.

8. *Wa* 84, 61.

9. E. E. Cummings, "Introduction" to 1938 *Collected Poems, Poems 1923–1954* (New York: Harcourt, 1954), 331.

10. *CD* 88, 84.

11. *Wa* 71.

12. *Wa* 155.

13. *J* 2:173–174; *J* 1:199, 347.

14. *Wa* 324–325.

15. William Ellery Channing II, "Walden," in *American Poetry: The Nineteenth Century*, ed. John Hollander, 2 vols. (New York: Library of America, 1993), 1:674.

Chapter 3

1. Alice Felt Tyler, *Freedom's Ferment: Phases of American Social History to 1860* (Minneapolis: University of Minnesota Press, 1944).

2. Octavius Brooks Frothingham, *Transcendentalism in New England: A History* (New York: G. P. Putnam, 1867), 134.

3. Ralph Waldo Emerson, *Journals and Miscellaneous Notebooks*, ed. William H. Gilman et al., 16 vols. (Cambridge, MA: Harvard University Press, 1960–82), 7:342.

4. Emerson, *Nature, The Collected Works of Ralph Waldo Emerson*, vol. 1: *Nature, Addresses, and Lectures*, ed. Alfred R. Ferguson (Cambridge, MA: Harvard University Press, 1971), 7, 56, 90; Emerson, "Self-Reliance," in *Collected Works of RWE: Essays, First Series*, ed. Alfred R. Ferguson and Jean Ferguson Carr (Cambridge, MA: Harvard University Press, 1979), 28.

5. *J* 1:5.

6. Emerson, "Thoreau," in *Collected Works of RWE*, vol. 10: *Uncollected Prose Writings*, ed. Ronald A. Bosco and Joel Myerson (Cambridge, MA: Harvard University Press, 2013), 431, 429.

7. Emerson, "Politics," in *Collected Works of RWE*, vol. 3: *Essays, Second Series*, ed. Alfred R. Ferguson and Jean Ferguson Carr (Cambridge, MA: Harvard University Press, 1983), 126, 122.

8. *Wa* 98. Compare Emerson, "Experience," *Essays, Second Series*, 29.

9. Alcott, *The Doctrine and Discipline of Human Culture* (1836), rpt. *The American Transcendentalists: Essential Writings*, ed. Lawrence Buell (New York: Modern Library, 2006), 71.

10. Parker, *A Discourse of the Transient and Permanent in Christianity* (1841), rpt. *The American Transcendentalists: Essential Writings*, 168.

11. Laura Dassow Walls, *Henry David Thoreau: A Life* (Chicago: University of Chicago Press, 2017), 209.

12. Emerson, *Nature*, 45.

13. Ibid., 21, 18.

14. *Wa* 317–318.

15. Dickens, *American Notes* (1842; rpt. Oxford: Oxford University Press, 1997), 57.

16. Emerson, *Journals and Miscellaneous Notebooks*, 16:21–22.

Chapter 4

1. *The Correspondence of Henry David Thoreau*, ed. Robert N. Hudspeth, 3 vols. (Princeton, NJ: Princeton University Press, 2013), 1:308.

2. *J* 1:85–86; *Wa* 23, 102.

3. *J* 4:412.

4. *Wa* 16, 252.

5. Thoreau, "Sic Vita" (1841), rpt. *American Poetry: The Nineteenth Century*, ed. John Hollander, 2 vols. (New York: Library of America, 1993), 1:662.

6. *J* 3:62; *J* 4:50.

7. Thoreau, *A Week on the Concord and Merrimack Rivers*, ed. Carl Hovde (Princeton, NJ: Princeton University Press, 1980), 277.

8. Max Oelschlaeger, *The Idea of Wilderness: From Prehistory to the Age of Ecology* (New Haven: Yale University Press, 1991), 149.

9. *Wa* 317.

10. Thoreau, *The Maine Woods*, ed. Joseph J. Moldenhauer (Princeton, NJ: Princeton University Press, 1972), 156.

11. Thoreau, *Cape Cod*, ed. Joseph J. Moldenhauer (Princeton, NJ: Princeton University Press, 1988), 9.

12. Ibid., 179–197.

13. *J* 2:446.

14. François Specq, "Poetics of Thoreau's Journal and Postmodern Aesthetics," in *Thoreauvian Modernities: Transatlantic Conversations on an American Icon*, ed. Specq, Laura Dassow Walls, and Michel Granger (Athens: University of Georgia Press, 2013), 221; Branka Arsić, *Bird Relics: Grief and Vitalism in Thoreau* (Cambridge, MA: Harvard University Press, 2016), 99.

15. Malcolm Clemens Young, *The Spiritual Journal of Henry David Thoreau* (Macon, GA: Mercer University Press, 2009); Robert Thorson, *Walden's Shore: Henry David Thoreau and Nineteenth-Century Science* (Cambridge, MA: Harvard University Press, 2014); Sharon Cameron, *Writing Nature: Henry Thoreau's Journal* (New York: Oxford University Press, 1985).

16. *J1906* 10:226–228.

17. *J1906* 10:234; *J* 3:377.

Chapter 5

1. William Ellery Channing II, *Thoreau: The Poet-Naturalist* (Boston: Roberts Brothers, 1873).

2. *The Correspondence of Henry David Thoreau*, ed. Robert N. Hudspeth, 3 vols. (Princeton, NJ: Princeton University Press, 2018), 2:3.

3. Reed Gochberg, "In 19th Century New England, This Amateur Geologist Created Her Own Cabinet of Curiosities," *Smithsonian Magazine*, November 19, 2021, https://www.smithsonianmag.com/history/in-19th-century-new-england-this-amateur-geologist-created-her-own-cabinet-of-curiosities-180979083/, consulted July 27, 2022. Compare Lynn L. Merrill, *The Romance of Victorian Natural History* (New York: Oxford University Press, 1989).

4. Thoreau, *Excursions*, ed. Joseph J. Moldenhauer (Princeton, NJ: Princeton University Press, 2002), 5, 27.

5. *J1906* 13:149, 151.

6. Charles J. Jackson, *Proceedings of the Boston Society of Natural History* 9 (1862): 71.

7. Laura Dassow Walls, *Thoreau: A Life* (Chicago: University of Chicago Press, 2017), 439.

8. *J* 5:113; 8:91, 245; *J1906* 12:113.

9. *J* 3:380.

10. *J* 5:469–470.

11. *Correspondence of Henry David Thoreau*, 2:151.

12. *J1906* 12:175.

13. *J1906* 12:91.

14. Walls, *Thoreau: A Life*, 339.

15. Thoreau, *The Maine Woods*, ed. Joseph J. Moldenhauer (Princeton, NJ: Princeton University Press, 1972), 290.

16. Emerson, "Thoreau," in *Collected Works of Ralph Waldo Emerson*, vol. 10: *Uncollected Prose Writings*, ed. Ronald A. Bosco and Joel Myerson (Cambridge, MA: Harvard University Press, 2013), 431.

17. Robert M. Thorson, *Walden's Shore: Henry David Thoreau and Nineteenth-Century Science* (Cambridge, MA: Harvard University Press, 2014), 204, 130.

18. Thorson, *The Boatman* (Cambridge, MA: Harvard University Press, 2017), 19.

19. Thoreau, "The Dispersion of Seeds," in *Faith in a Seed: The Dispersion of Seeds and Other Late Natural History Writings*, ed. Bradley P. Dean (Washington, DC: Island Press, 1993), 169.

20. Robert D. Richardson Jr., *Henry David Thoreau: A Life of the Mind* (Berkeley: University of California Press, 1986), 292.

Chapter 6

1. Thoreau, "Of the duty, inconvenience and dangers of *conformity*" [Harvard assigned theme], in *Early Essays and Miscellanies*, ed. Joseph J. Moldenhauer and Edwin Moser (Princeton: Princeton University Press, 1975), 106; Emerson, "Thoreau," *The Collected Works of Ralph Waldo Emerson*, vol. 10: *Uncollected Prose Writings*, ed. Ronald A. Bosco and Joel Myerson (Cambridge, MA: Harvard University Press, 2013), 416–417.

2. Emerson, "Thoreau," 415–416.

3. Laura Dassow Walls, *Thoreau: A Life* (Chicago: University of Chicago Press, 2017), 456.

4. Emerson, "War," *Aesthetic Papers*, ed. Elizabeth Peabody (Boston: Putnam, 1849), 36–50.

5. Sumner, "The True Grandeur of Nations," in *Orations and Speeches* (Boston: Ticknor, Reed, & Fields, 1850), 11.

6. CD 65; Thoreau, [review of speech by] "Wendell Phillips Before the Concord Lyceum," in *Reform Papers*, ed. Wendell Glick (Princeton, NJ: Princeton University Press, 1973), 61.

7. CD 74, 75; CD 65.

8. *Wa* 171.

9. *CD* 68.

10. Thoreau, "Slavery in Massachusetts," *Reform Papers*, 101, 104.

11. *Wa* 7.

12. Thoreau, "A Plea for Captain John Brown," *Reform Papers*, 125.

13. *CD* 84; "Plea for Captain John Brown," 133, 137.

14. *The Correspondence of Henry David Thoreau*, vol. 2: *1849–1856*, ed. Robert N. Hudspeth (Princeton, NJ: Princeton University Press, 2018), 471.

15. Sandra Harbert Petrulionis, *To Set This World Aright: The Antislavery Movement in Thoreau's Concord* (Ithaca, NY: Cornell University Press, 2006), 137.

16. Thoreau, "The Last Days of John Brown," *Reform Papers*, 153.

17. Thoreau, "Plea for Captain John Brown," 112, 115.

18. Thoreau, "Slavery in Massachusetts," 108, 109.

19. *Wa* 167; *J1906* 9: 36.

20. Nancy Armstrong, "Thoreau's Militant Conscience," *Political Theory* 9 (1981): 105.

21. George Kateb, *The Inner Ocean: Individualism and Democratic Culture* (Ithaca, NY: Cornell University Press, 1992), 78; Leigh Kathryn Jurco, "Thoreau's Critique of Democracy," in *A Political Companion to Henry David Thoreau*, ed. Jack Turner (Lexington: University Press of Kentucky, 2009), 86.

22. Jonathan McKenzie, *The Political Thought of Henry David Thoreau: Privatism and the Practice of Philosophy* (Lexington: University Press of Kentucky, 2016),

135; Hannah Arendt, *Crises of the Republic* (New York: Harcourt, Brace, Jovanovich, 1972), 60.

23. *Wa* 4; Stanley Cavell, *The Senses of Walden: An Expanded Edition* (San Francisco: North Point Press, 1981), 85.

24. Thoreau, "Life without Principle," *Reform Papers*, 174.

25. Thoreau, "Life without Principle," 175, 178.

Chapter 7

1. E. O. Wilson, *The Future of Life* (New York: Alfred A. Knopf, 2002), xx.

2. Percy Bysshe Shelley, "A Defense of Poetry," in *Shelley's Poetry and Prose*, ed. Donald H. Reiman and Neil Fraistat (New York: Norton, 2002), 535; Walt Whitman, *Notebooks and Unpublished Prose Fragments*, ed. Edward F. Grier, 6 vols. (New York: New York University Press, 1964), 1:353.

3. *J1906* 11:324; *Wa* 153; *J* 1: 355; Thoreau, *A Week on the Concord and Merrimack Rivers*, ed. Carl Hovde (Princeton, NJ: Princeton University Press, 1980), 73, 64.

4. Thoreau, "A Yankee in Canada," in *Excursions*, ed. Joseph J. Moldenhauer (Princeton, NJ: Princeton University Press, 2007), 88.

5. Thoreau, *A Week*, 66; Alan Hodder, *Thoreau's Ecstatic Witness* (New Haven: Yale University Press, 2001), 139.

6. Thoreau, *A Week*, 144.

7. *Wa* 311, 14, 74, 153.

8. Thoreau, *Reform Papers*, ed. Wendell Glick (Princeton, NJ: Princeton University Press, 1973), 76, 173, 103.

9. *Wa* 107, 150.

10. Caleb Smith, *Thoreau's Axe: Distraction and Discipline in American Culture* (Princeton, NJ: Princeton University Press, 2023), 177.

11. *J* 2:159, 175; *Wa* 321, 332, 207.

12. *Wa* 67, 112, 323.

13. *The Correspondence of Henry David Thoreau*, ed. Robert N. Hudspeth, 3 vols. (Princeton, NJ: Princeton University Press, 2018), 2:489.

14. Bradford Angier and Vera Angier, *At Home in the Woods* (New York: Sheridan House, 1972), 11.

15. Alda Balthrop-Lewis, *Thoreau's Religion: Walden Woods, Social Justice, and the Politics of Asceticism* (Cambridge: Cambridge University Press, 2021), 207.

16. *Wa* 97.

17. *J* 4:55; *Wa* 193, 111.

18. *The Collected Works of Ralph Waldo Emerson*, vol. 1: *Nature, Addresses, Lectures*, ed. Alfred R. Ferguson (Cambridge, MA: Harvard University Press, 1971), 10.

19. *Wa* 138, 306–307.

20. Laura Dassow Walls, "A Material Faith: Thoreau's Terrenial Turn," in *Dispersion: Thoreau and Vegetal Thought*, ed. Branka Arsić (New York: Bloomsbury, 2021), 37–58.

21. *Wa* 97, 220.

22. *J1906* 9:217–218; *Correspondence of Henry David Thoreau*, 2:43, 404.

23. Branka Arsić, *Bird Relics: Grief and Vitalism in Thoreau* (Cambridge, MA: Harvard University Press, 2016), 121–129.

24. Emerson, *Nature*, 39.

25. Thoreau, "Dispersion of Seeds," in *Faith in a Seed*, ed. Bradley P. Dean (Washington, DC: Island Press 1993), 50.

26. *Wa* 134.

27. David Robinson, *Natural Life: Thoreau's Worldly Transcendentalism* (Ithaca, NY: Cornell University Press, 2004), 181, 147.

28. Thoreau, "Life without Principle," in *Reform Papers*, 161; *Wa* 332.

29. *Correspondence of Henry David Thoreau*, 2:55.

30. *J1906* 9:45–46.

31. *Daniel Ricketson and His Friends*, ed. Anna Ricketson and Walton Ricketson (Boston: Houghton Mifflin, 1902), 137.

32. *Journals and Miscellaneous Notebooks of Ralph Waldo Emerson*, ed. William Gilman et al., 16 vols. (Cambridge, MA: Harvard University Press, 1960–82), 15:246.

33. Quoted in Walter Harding, *The Days of Henry Thoreau*, rev. ed. (Princeton, NJ: Princeton University Press, 1982), 464–465.

34. Orwell, "Reflections on Gandhi," in *A Collection of Essays* (Garden City, NY: Doubleday, 1954), 177.

35. *Wa* 216; Jonathan Krakauer, *Into the Wild* (New York: Anchor Books, 1996), 47.

FURTHER READING

EDITIONS OF THOREAU'S WORK

The standard edition, still in progress, is *The Writings of Henry David Thoreau* (Princeton, NJ: Princeton University Press, 1971–), 18 vols. to date. As of 2023, it includes *Walden, A Week on the Concord and Merrimack Rivers, The Maine Woods, Cape Cod, Early Essays and Miscellanies, Reform Papers, Excursions*, the *Journal* through 1854 (8 vols.), *Correspondence* through 1856 (2 vols.), and *Translations*. Whenever possible I cite this edition.

The entire *Journal* is online at http://thoreau.library.ucsb.edu/writings_journals.html.

For those who prefer print, a reasonably complete but cosmetically edited text is *The Journal of Henry David Thoreau*, 14 vols., ed. Bradford Torrey and Francis Allen (Boston: Houghton Mifflin, 1906).

For Thoreau's later letters, see *The Correspondence of Henry David Thoreau*, ed. Walter Harding and Carl Bode (New York: New York University Press, 1968).

A reliable, inexpensive edition of the four books Thoreau completed in his lifetime, or nearly so, is *Henry David Thoreau: A Week, Walden, The Maine Woods, Cape Cod*, ed. Robert F. Sayre (New York: Library of America, 1985). *Walden, "Civil Disobedience," and Other Writings*, ed. William Rossi (New York: W. W. Norton, 2008), is a scrupulously edited collection of Thoreau's most essential works with notes, reviews, and critical essays.

The best available collection of Thoreau's poems is *Henry David Thoreau: Collected Essays and Poems*, ed. Elizabeth Hall Witherell (New York: Library of America, 2001).

For Thoreau's natural history writings, in addition to *Excursions*, see *Faith in a Seed: The Dispersion of Seeds and Other Late Natural History Writings*, ed. Bradley P. Dean (Washington, DC: Island Press, 1993); and *Wild Fruits: Thoreau's Rediscovered Last Manuscript*, ed. Dean (New York: W. W. Norton, 1999).

BIOGRAPHIES

The best biography of Thoreau in English is Laura Dassow Walls, *Henry David Thoreau: A Life* (Chicago: University of Chicago Press, 2017). Readers of German will also value Dieter Schulz, *Henry David Thoreau: Wege eines amerikanisches Schriftstellers* (Heidelberg: Mattes, 2017). An important supplement to both is Robert D. Richardson Jr.'s intellectual biography, *Henry David Thoreau: A Life of the Mind* (Berkeley: University of California Press, 1986). Still helpful on some details is Walter Harding, *The Days of Henry Thoreau*, rev. ed. (Princeton, NJ: Princeton University Press, 1982; orig. 1965). For an illuminating collection of biographical glimpses by those who knew Thoreau, see *Thoreau in His Own Time: A Biographical Chronicle of His Life*, ed. Sandra Petrulionis (Iowa City: University of Iowa Press, 2012).

INTERPRETATIVE BIOGRAPHICAL-CRITICAL STUDIES

Of the many scholarly books that encompass the whole arc of Thoreau's life and career, of particular value are Robert Milder, *Reimagining Thoreau* (New York: Cambridge University Press, 1995); David Robinson, *Natural Life: Thoreau's Worldly Transcendentalism* (Ithaca, NY: Cornell University Press, 2004); and Branka Arsić, *Bird Relics: Grief and Vitalism in Thoreau* (Cambridge, MA: Harvard University Press, 2017).

LITERARY THOREAU

On Thoreau's literary career as a whole, in addition to the three works listed above, see Stephen Fink, *Prophet in the Marketplace: Thoreau's Development as a Professional Writer* (Princeton, NJ: Princeton University Press, 1992).

Other important discussions of *Walden* as a work of creative imagination include Stanley Cavell, *The Senses of Walden: An Expanded Edition* (San Francisco: North Point Press, 1981), and Robert Sattelmeyer, "The Remaking of *Walden*," in *Writing the American Classics*, ed. James Barbour and Tom Quirk (Chapel Hill: University of North Carolina Press, 1990), 53–78.

For Thoreau and travel writing traditions, John Aldrich Christie, *Thoreau as World Traveler* (New York: Columbia University Press, 1965), remains the source of first resort.

On Thoreau the lecturer, see Ronald Wesley Hoag, "Odd Man In: Thoreau, the Lyceum Movement, and the Lecture Circuit," in *Henry David Thoreau in Context*, ed. James S. Finley (Cambridge: Cambridge University Press, 2017).

On Thoreau's *Journal*, see especially Sharon Cameron, *Writing Nature: Henry Thoreau's Journal* (New York: Oxford University Press, 1985); H. Daniel Peck, *Thoreau's Morning Work: Memory and Perception in A Week on the Concord and Merrimack Rivers, the Journal, and Walden* (New Haven: Yale University Press, 1990); and François Specq, "Poetics of Thoreau's Journal and Postmodern Aesthetics," *Thoreauvian Modernities: Transatlantic Conversations on an American Icon*, ed. Specq, Laura Dassow Walls, and Michel Granger (Athens: University of Georgia Press, 3013), 219–233.

NATURE AND ENVIRONMENT: THEORY, PRACTICE, INFLUENCE

On Thoreau's theory of nature, see Jane Bennett, *Thoreau's Nature: Ethics, Politics, and the Wild* (Thousand Oaks, CA: Sage, 1994). On Thoreau and the theory/practice/history of nature writing: Lawrence Buell, *The Environmental Imagination: Thoreau, Nature Writing, and the Formation of American Culture* (Cambridge, MA: Harvard University Press 1995). On Thoreau's legacy for environmentalism: Daniel B. Botkin, *No Man's Garden: Thoreau and a New Vision for Civilization and Nature* (Washington, DC: Island Press, 2001); and Richard W. Judd, *Finding Thoreau: The Meaning of Nature in the Making of an Environmental Icon* (Amherst: University of Massachusetts Press, 2018).

ETHNOGRAPHY; BIOLOGICAL, PHYSICAL, AND APPLIED SCIENCE

On Thoreau's "Indian Books" and interest in American aboriginal culture, see Robert Sayre, *Thoreau and the American Indians* (Princeton, NJ: Princeton University Press, 1977); and John J. Kucich, "Native America," in *Henry David Thoreau in Context*, 196–204.

On Thoreau as life-scientist and thinker, see Laura Dassow Walls, *Seeing New Worlds: Henry David Thoreau and 19th Century Natural Science* (Madison: University of Wisconsin Press, 1995); Richard B. Primack, *Walden Warming: Climate Change Comes to Thoreau's Woods* (Chicago: University of Chicago Press, 2014); and William Rossi, "Evolution," in *Henry David Thoreau in Context*, 279–287. On Thoreau as physical scientist: Robert

Thorson, *Walden's Shore: Henry David Thoreau and Nineteenth-Century Science* (Cambridge, MA: Harvard University Press, 2014).

On Thoreau as engineer and applied scientist, see Patrick Chura, *Thoreau the Land Surveyor* (Gainesville: University Press of Florida, 2010); Robert Thorson, *The Boatman: Henry Thoreau's River Years* (Cambridge, MA: Harvard University Press, 2017); and Laura Dassow Walls, "Technology," in *Henry David Thoreau in Context*, 165–174.

POLITICS

On "Civil Disobedience," see Lawrence A. Rosenwald, "The Theory, Practice, and Influence of Thoreau's Civil Disobedience," in *A Historical Guide to Henry David Thoreau* (New York: Oxford University Press, 2000), 153–179; Robert A. Gross, "Quiet War with the State: Henry David Thoreau and Civil Disobedience," *Yale Review* 9 (October 2005): 1–17; and Wai Chee Dimock, "Global Civil Society: Thoreau on Three Continents," in Dimock, *Through Other Continents: American Literature Across Deep Time* (Princeton, NJ: Princeton University Press, 2006), 7–22.

On Thoreau's political thought and influence in general: George Kateb, *The Inner Ocean: Individualism and Democratic Culture* (Ithaca, NY: Cornell University Press, 1992); *A Political Companion to Henry David Thoreau*, ed. Jack Turner (Lexington: University Press of Kentucky, 2009); Jonathan McKenzie, *The Political Thought of Henry David Thoreau: Privatism and the Practice of Philosophy* (Lexington: University Press of Kentucky, 2016); and Bob Pepperman Taylor, *Lessons from Walden: Thoreau and the Crisis of American Democracy* (Notre Dame, IN: Notre Dame University Press, 2020).

ETHICS, PHILOSOPHY, RELIGION

On Thoreau as philosophic, ethical, and religious thinker, see Cavell, *Senses of Walden*; Philip Cafaro, *Thoreau's Living Ethics: Walden and the Pursuit of Virtue* (Athens: University of Georgia Press, 2000); Alfred Tauber, *Henry David Thoreau and the Moral Agency of Knowing* (Berkeley: University of California Press, 2001); Alan D. Hodder, *Thoreau's Ecstatic Witness* (New Haven: Yale University Press, 2001); and Audrey Raden, *When I Came to Die: Process and Prophecy in Thoreau's Vision of Dying* (Amherst: University of Massachusetts Press, 2017).

BIOGRAPHICAL AND HISTORICAL BACKGROUNDS AND CONTEXTS

On the history of Transcendentalism, see Barbara Packer, "The Transcendentalists," in *The Cambridge History of American Literature*, ed. Sacvan Bercovich (New York: Cambridge University Press, 1995), 329–604, rpt. as *The Transcendentalists* (Athens: University of Georgia Press, 2007); Philip Gura, *American Transcendentalism: A History* (New York: Hill & Wang, 2007); and Peter Wirzbicki, *Fighting for the Higher Law: Black and White Transcendentalists Against Slavery* (Philadelphia: University of Pennsylvania Press, 2021). A convenient anthology with introductory overviews is *The American Transcendentalists: Essential Writings*, ed. Lawrence Buell (New York: Modern Library, 2006).

On the Emerson–Thoreau relationship: Harmon Smith, *My Friend, My Friend: The Story of Thoreau's Relationship with Emerson* (Amherst: University of Massachusetts Press, 1999); Jeffrey S. Cramer, *Solid Seasons: The Friendship of Henry David Thoreau and Ralph Waldo Emerson* (Berkeley, CA: Counterpoint, 2019), which reprints their essays on friendship and comments on each other; Robert Sattelmeyer, "'When He Became My Enemy': Emerson and Thoreau, 1848–1849," *New England Quarterly* 62 (1989): 187–204; and Lawrence Buell, "Transcendental Friendship: An Oxymoron?," in *Emerson and Thoreau: Figures of Friendship*, ed. John T. Lysaker and William Rossi (Bloomington: Indiana University Press, 2010), 17–32.

On the history of Thoreau's Concord, see Robert Gross, *The Transcendentalists and Their World* (New York: Farrar, Straus and Giroux, 2021); Sandra Herbert Petrulionis, *To Set This World Aright: The Antislavery Movement in Thoreau's Concord* (Ithaca, NY: Cornell University Press, 2006); W. Barksdale Maynard, *Walden Pond: A History* (New York: Oxford University Press, 2004); and Elise Lemire, *Black Walden* (Philadelphia: University of Pennsylvania Press, 2009).

Other studies that helpfully situate Thoreau in relation to Western and Asian intellectual, cultural, and social history include David Shi, *The Simple Life: Plain Living and High Thinking in American Culture* (New York: Oxford University Press, 1985); Arthur Versluis, *American Transcendentalism and Asian Religions* (New York: Oxford University Press, 1993); George P. Landow, *Elegant Jeremiahs: The Sage from Carlyle to Mailer* (Ithaca, NY: Cornell University Press, 1986); William A. Gleason, *The Leisure Ethic: Work and Play in American Literature, 1840–1940* (Stanford: Stanford University Press, 1999); Lance Newman, *Our Common Dwelling: Henry Thoreau, Transcendentalism, and the Class Politics of Nature* (New York: Palgrave Macmillan, 2005); Michael T. Gilmore, *The War on Words: Slavery, Race, and Free Speech in American Literature* (Chicago: University of Chicago Press, 2010); and Reed Gochberg, *Useful Objects: Museums, Science, and Literature in Nineteenth-Century America* (New York: Oxford University Press, 2021).

INDEX

Figures are indicated by *f* following the page number. For entries under "Thoreau: Works" especially substantial discussions are listed in bold